GOD SPACE

"As I've spoken to thousands of people regarding externally focused living, the missing piece I've identified is the type of conversation that helps turn good deeds and good will into good news for this generation. Through genuine concern, coupled with curiosity and questions, Doug, through Scripture, story, and experiences (both positive and negative) presents attractive and compelling ways to engage others in conversations that change lives for eternity."

—Eric Swanson
Co-Author of *The Externally Focused Church* and *Living a Life on Loan*

"Conversations involving evangelism are increasingly difficult—for seeker and would-be evangelist alike. Lots of us have tried to make a contribution to this challenge. Doug Pollock has actually done so. *God Space* is wide-ranging but easily grasped; honest to the challenge, but loaded with doable actions and thus hope."

—Todd Hunter
Church Planter, Anglican Mission in the Americas; Former Executive Director, Alpha USA; and Former President, Vineyard USA

"When we share with another our relationship with Jesus, we share the most precious gift we could ever receive. Why are we often reluctant, even fearful, to share this wonderful gift? Part of the answer must lie in the fact that most of us have never taken the time to intentionally prepare to be effective witnesses for Jesus, the lover of our souls. Doug Pollock has drawn from his years of compassion for the lost to help any follower of Jesus become a more effective laborer in the harvest. This book guides us to the awareness that every encounter is a divine opportunity to sow a seed of the gospel and, through practical examples and useful tools, equips us to share the hope that lies within us."

—David Long
President, OMS International

"Doug Pollock's *God Space* is a jam-packed guidebook on the new apologetic: listening, noticing, and serving while leading others to the mercy of God. The chapter with "99 wondering questions" is invaluable for those of us weary of parroting formulaic answers in the oft-typical sales approach of evangelical Christianity. Doug is a practitioner, not a theoretician; these ideas and stories are borne from real-life experiences. That alone makes it well worth the read!"

—Dave Workman
Author of *The Outward-Focused Life*; Senior Pastor, Vineyard Community Church, Cincinnati, Ohio

"What would happen if Christians left their 'clubs' and went out into the world to create high-grace places where conversation flowed freely and people could voice their questions about life? In *God Space,* author Doug Pollock offers readers his experience and real-life stories of doing exactly that. As he actively wonders with people, we are drawn into his passion for reaching people far from God. But Pollock does something few writers do—he leaves us believing that we, too, can wonder into people's hearts and ultimately help them wonder their way to God. Doug Pollock has given the church an authentic and invaluable tool for reaching and connecting to the hearts of people."

> —Lindy Lowry
> Senior Editor,
> Outreach magazine

"If you are looking for a down-to-earth coach to give you the practical help you need to make the most of the encounters God brings your way, Doug Pollock is one of the best there is. His insights are warm, witty—and so true! If you apply the teaching of this book, you will never need to attend another evangelism training program. Guaranteed."

> —Howard Webb
> Love Your Neighbour Network,
> New Zealand

"God Space: It's a place where day-to-day relationships and remarkably refreshing spiritual conversations meet. In *God Space,* Doug Pollock provides everything we need to engage with others in seeking, asking, and knocking on God's door to get the everlasting directions we all need."

> —Dave Ping
> CEO, Equipping Ministries
> International; Co-author of *Outflow*

"I've had the privilege of traveling with Doug and seeing him create God Space in person. Doug is a practitioner who passionately provokes and nudges the people who cross his path to question, to examine, to wonder, and to journey forward toward Jesus. The timeless concepts in each chapter are eye-opening, learnable, practical, and doable, which helps readers to apply and experience God Space for themselves. I know, because I've had the opportunity to teach God Space in a small group setting. I can say without hesitation God Space works!"

> —Steve Bowen
> Outreach Pastor, Vineyard Church,
> Dayton, Ohio

GOD SPACE

WHERE SPIRITUAL CONVERSATIONS HAPPEN NATURALLY

DOUG POLLOCK

Group

Loveland, Colorado

group.com

Group resources actually work!

This Group resource incorporates our R.E.A.L. approach to ministry. It reinforces a growing friendship with Jesus, encourages long-term learning, and results in life transformation, because it's

Relational
Learner-to-learner interaction enhances learning and builds Christian friendships.

Experiential
What learners experience through discussion and action sticks with them up to 9 times longer than what they simply hear or read.

Applicable
The aim of Christian education is to equip learners to be both hearers and doers of God's Word.

Learner-based
Learners understand and retain more when the learning process takes into consideration how they learn best.

GOD SPACE
WHERE SPIRITUAL CONVERSATIONS HAPPEN NATURALLY
Doug Pollock

"How Well Do You Listen?" on pages 56-57 and "Reflective Listening Phrases" beginning on page 60 are reprinted with the permission of Equipping Ministries International, Cincinnati, Ohio, equippingministries.org
The "99 Wondering Questions" beginning on page 108 are adapted from *Irresistible Evangelism* copyright © Steve Sjogren, Dave Ping, and Doug Pollock.
Parts of Chapter 8 were originally published in the March/April 2007 issue of Outreach magazine and are reprinted by permission.
Parts of Chapter 10 were originally published in the July/August 2005 issue of Outreach magazine and are reprinted by permission.

Visit our website: **group.com**

Credits
Senior Editor: Candace McMahan
Editor: Carl Simmons
Chief Creative Officer: Joani Schultz
Copy Editor: Zach Carlson

Art Director: Paul Povolni
Cover Photographer: Rodney Stewart
Book Designer: Jean Bruns
Production Manager: DeAnne Lear

Library of Congress Cataloging-in-Publication Data
Pollock, Doug, 1957-
  God space : naturally creating room for spiritual conversations / Doug Pollock.
    p. cm.
  ISBN 978-0-7644-3871-4 (pbk. : alk. paper)
  1. Evangelistic work. I. Title.
  BV3790.P595 2009
  269'.2--dc22
                            2009014082

20 19 18 17   19 18 17 16

Printed in the United States of America.

GOD|SPACE

Contents

Dedication

This book is dedicated to Christ-followers all over the world who long to see the quality and quantity of their spiritual conversations increase in natural and doable ways.

It is also dedicated to leaders who long to see God's people leave the church on Sunday to be the church from Monday through Saturday. It's my desire that these tangible expressions of how to live outwardly focused lives in an inwardly focused world will help you create churches without walls, raising up people who are not only giving to missions, but are also given to mission.

Acknowledgments

Thanks to my teammates, who for the past 25 years have sacrificially given so that I would be free to bring God's good news to people in 36 different countries, almost every state in the U.S., and six of seven continents. Your ongoing commitment has enabled me to have a wealth of experiences from which to write this book. Thus far, our partnership has paved the way for multitudes of people to discover the kingdom of God. Only God knows how many more will come to know him through the spiritual conversations sparked by this book.

A special word of thanks to Denny and Peggy Hicks for allowing me to use their cabin in the country to finish my writing, and to all my friends, too numerous to mention, who provided valuable feedback in refining the book you now have in your hands.

I'd also like to recognize Panera Bread bakery-cafes around the country. You get my vote for the best place to write a book while on the road. I love your food and atmosphere.

Thanks as well to the folks at Group Publishing, who year after year create avenues for people who think and care deeply about advancing the kingdom of God. I am grateful for our partnership. I especially want to thank my editor, Candace McMahan, who prayed me through the ups and downs of writing this book.

Finally, I thank my wife, Martha, and my two sons, David and Jonathan. Writing this book required me to set apart time from each of you that I can never have back. I'm hoping that you'll each find something in here to help you in the multitudes of relational connections you'll have over your lifetimes. It will make the trade-off so much more worthwhile. Thanks for your love and support through it all.

Author's Note: The stories you will read throughout this book really happened. Because of the personal nature of these stories, I have changed the names out of sensitivity and respect to all involved.

Introduction

If you want to increase the quantity and quality of your spiritual conversations, or don't feel competent or confident enough to even begin a spiritual conversation, read on. You'll find practical stories that reveal solid biblical principles for engaging people in spiritual conversations.

If you're looking for a formula, a method, or the latest evangelistic road map, you won't find it here. I've been there and done that! Methods and road maps, while useful for a while, eventually become obsolete as times change. If you want to stay spiritually relevant, then you must focus on that which is eternal. God's timeless truths never change.

Therefore, I'd like you to imagine that you're holding God's GPS in your hand. Regardless of when you pick this book up to read it, or where you live in the world, God's everlasting principles herein will never fail to guide you as you seek to make him known in your relational encounters.

If you want to read little and apply much, if you prefer the practical over the theoretical, I pray you'll find this book to be everything you're looking for. You'll find prayers to offer, books to read, questions to answer, movies and clips to watch, Scriptures to meditate on, quotes to memorize, faith experiments to try, and applications to make. As you use these ideas, you'll begin to make the journey from information to transformation.

So if you're ready to naturally create room—God Space—for spiritual conversations to happen in your everyday life, pour a cup of coffee and start reading. Before long, you'll begin to realize just how hungry people are to talk about God—and how you can help those conversations to happen!

GOD

CHAPTER 1

Creating God Space

Paul and Lisa, a young married couple, were heading home to celebrate the holiday season with Lisa's side of the family. Three years earlier, after a rocky first year of marriage, Paul and Lisa had realized they needed something greater than themselves to make their marriage work. They discovered an older married couple who helped them realize that if Jesus were in control of their lives, he could help the two of them become one.

As they grew in their newfound faith, they began to realize that no one else in their entire family believed in Jesus the way they did. Nevertheless, neither Paul nor Lisa felt confident or competent enough to talk about the faith that had turned their lives and marriage around. They had the desire, and they even saw the need, but they didn't know how to bring up their faith in a natural way, so they didn't. However, they were determined to change all that, this Christmas. As they neared their destination, Paul and Lisa's sense of inadequacy and fear of failure drove them into a time of prayer.

If you'd been sitting in the back seat of their car that day, and Paul and Lisa had turned around after their prayer time and asked you for advice on how to bring up the topic of faith, what would you have told them? How do you start a spiritual conversation with family, friends, or co-workers without turning them off?

Keep thinking about this question, for it's a very important one. But for now, let's dive back into our story to find out what Paul and Lisa did.

On Christmas Day, after all the gifts were opened, Paul and Lisa were casually sitting around, catching up with Lisa's younger sister, Karen. Paul and Lisa had heard that Karen was into some kind of New Age religion she had

discovered through friends in college. When Paul and Lisa asked her how things were going, Karen excitedly told them that she was on a spiritual high due to an angel that had recently appeared to her in a dream.

This was the opportunity Paul and Lisa had been looking and praying for. Before Karen even had a chance to share what the angel had told her, Lisa hijacked the conversation. She passionately informed her sister that Scripture says the devil masquerades as the angel of light—that she didn't know what she was messing around with.

Once Lisa had finished her sermonette, she tagged out, and Paul tagged in. He made sure Karen understood that her New Age religion was akin to witchcraft. Paul felt a surge of confidence and power as he pronounced other truths he was convinced Karen needed to hear.

After Paul and Lisa finished double-teaming Karen, the room was filled with an awkward silence. The conversation was over before it ever began. Karen got up and left the room. Paul and Lisa had wounded her so deeply that Karen refused to speak to them the rest of the holiday season. What's more, when Karen told the rest of the family how she had been disrespected, parented, judged, and essentially labeled as a witch, a family verdict was quickly reached. Paul and Lisa were now sentenced to wear the scarlet F (reserved for religious Fanatics) in the family.

Paul and Lisa drove home defeated and discouraged. The very thing they had feared the most had happened. This experience made it easy for them to become a part of the silent majority who keep their faith to themselves.

Karen and the rest of Lisa's family, on the other hand, came to an entirely different conclusion. They decided that the only way to have a safe conversation with a Christian is to make sure you say things you know they'll agree with—otherwise you'll be told why you're wrong and they're right. Rather than risk another awkward outcome, the whole family agreed not to talk about religion around Paul and Lisa again. Paul and Lisa's good intentions produced nothing more than hurt feelings, and a resolve on both sides to leave spiritual conversations alone.

A SAFE PLACE

I often wonder what would happen if—instead of all-too-common occurrences like the one above—the body of Christ could create low-risk, high-grace places for people to pursue their need to have spiritual conversations. According to Ecclesiastes 3:11, God has given us all an inner drive to know and be known by him. St. Augustine so brilliantly captured this thought when he wrote in his *Confessions*, "Our heart is not quiet until it rests in Thee." Where does an unquiet heart like Karen's go these days to safely share this yearning to know and be known by the Creator?

For most Christians, the answer is a no-brainer: It's the local church, of course! Unfortunately, this is not the word on the street. For many who grew up outside the walls of the church, going to church is a scary proposition.

I was reminded of this recently. I met the owner of a Japanese steakhouse in Fort Collins, Colorado, through a mutual friend. He came over to my friend's house to play pingpong. We were having such a good time that when he asked me what I did for a living, I did something I rarely do with a stranger: I invited him to come to church with me the next morning. I explained that I had been invited to Fort Collins to preach at a church, and if he wanted to experience firsthand what I do for a living, he was welcome to come join me. In strongly accented English, he quickly replied, "Oh, no, Mr. Doug, I too full of sin." My heart broke to hear him so eloquently express in broken English what millions have made abundantly clear. The church has become a scary place for people who are "too full of sin."

RAISING THE BAR—BY LOWERING IT

For many, going to church is as scary as going to a hard-core biker bar might be to Christians. This point became crystal clear to me in Idaho several years ago.

I was invited to do a workshop in a small town north of Boise by several local churches that were trying to figure out how to effectively reach their community. After a couple of hours of teaching on Friday night, I challenged everyone in the audience to head down to the local bar with my wife and me to apply what we'd just learned.

I was shocked by the response. Only one hand was raised. The pastor responsible for arranging my visit knew I wasn't going to let *him* off the hook, so it was no surprise to see *his* hand. As I probed to understand why these good-hearted people had unanimously declined my offer, they described the bar as a place for carousing, dirty jokes, swearing, drunkenness, smoking... the list went on until the "filthy five," "nasty nine," and "dirty dozen" had all been covered.

For many, going to church is as scary as going to
a hard-core biker bar might be to Christians.

After they finished sharing, I said, "It sounds like you're describing a bar to me. You didn't expect them to be singing 'Amazing Grace' and baptizing people with Bud Light down there, did you? Did Jesus call us to fish from the bank, or to swim with the fish, when he told us to go into all the world?"

My next question set them up: "How many of you would like to see the people at the bar come to church on Sunday morning?" All hands were raised.

I then asked, point-blank, "Who do you think is going to make the first move? If I go down to the bar and make the same invitation to them that I made to you, how many bar hoppers do you think would be willing to leave *their* 'club' to join *your* 'club' on Sunday morning? What would compel someone to give up what he likes to do most on Sunday morning, borrow a suit and tie, sing songs to somebody he can't see, listen to someone speak at him for 30 to 45 minutes about someone who lived more than 2,000 years ago, and then pay for the experience with something called an offering? How many takers do you think I'd have?"

I thought my stirring speech would surely move a few people to *be* the church down at the local bar that night, but no one budged. I'm opposed to using guilt and shame as crowbars to move God's people, so I ended by asking them to pray for their pastor, my wife, and me because we were going for it.

STEPPING OUT

As I walked away from the church, the Holy Spirit prompted me to ask my pastor friend if he had a video camera. I figured that the only way to help this group of Christians become more outwardly focused was to show them what an outward focus might look like.

We walked into the bar 15 minutes later. I introduced myself to a group of four, ranging from 18 to 21 years of age. I explained why I was in town and asked if they'd be willing to answer some questions about their experiences with the church. I encouraged them to keep it real because I'd be showing the video of our conversation the next day at my workshop. More than two hours later, the pastor, my wife, and I headed home from the bar after an exhilarating dialogue.

The flow of the conversation that evening went something like this: For 45 minutes I listened to this group share from their hearts about what had turned them off to church. As I listened, I got in touch with some of the things I had been wondering about, and at the appropriate time, I wondered out loud. These wondering questions (more about this in Chapter 6) stimulated their spiritual curiosity and opened the door for us to talk about spiritual matters. After an hour or so, they felt safe enough to ask their own questions about faith.

By the time our heart-to-heart exchange had ended, they asked me if it's possible to know for sure if they would end up in heaven. I had the privilege of sharing my faith story and the gospel with them. God's message had been hand-delivered to the appropriate spiritual address! (If you want to see for yourself what happened, you'll have to come to one of my workshops sometime. My schedule is posted at GodsGPS.com.)

The next morning, the people in my workshop were blown away by what they saw and heard on the video. God Space had been created in a place they had written off as the devil's playground. All I did was show up, jump on "God's teeter-totter" (more on that in Chapter 7), and let the Spirit lead.

THE FIRST MOVE

Both Christians and non-Christians have very real perceptions about one another that keep us from interacting in redeeming ways. It's been said that the only thing more difficult than getting the church to go to the world is getting the world to come to us. If showing up at each other's club is too scary for so many people, is there a way to create space in our daily interactions that might tear down some of the walls that keep us polarized?

I believe God wants Christians to make the first move. If I had chosen to stay at my club that night rather than head toward their club, nothing would have happened.

I firmly believe that if the American church doesn't grasp the implications of this need for Christians to move out of their comfort zones, 25 years from now we'll find ourselves in the same spiritual state as Europe and Canada. The local church used to be the heart and soul of American communities. Those days are slipping away fast, as church attendance continues to drop year after year nationwide. Today many churches need to face the cold, hard fact that if they closed their doors tomorrow, no one in the community

would miss them. It's as if we've forgotten that the early church in the book of Acts existed primarily for those who were *not* already Christ-followers.

Thom S. Rainer's research, documented in "Seven Sins of Dying Churches," supports this harsh reality. In a survey of churches across the U.S., he found that 95 percent of the ministries within the church are for church members alone. This statistic hit me like a baseball bat. I've had numerous experiences that have confirmed this inwardly focused mentality. The one that stands out best in my mind occurred during one of my workshops.

After I'd asked whether the church's budget reflected the heart of Jesus, one of the church leaders did some quick math to convert what I was saying into the bottom line. He had added the pastors' salaries, church employees' salaries, and all the other costs of keeping the church doors open. Then he'd divided that sum by the number of converts in the church's past year of ministry. He announced that in the past year, it had cost the church $440,000 per convert. Ouch! Now please understand that "everything that can be counted does not necessarily count; everything that counts cannot necessarily be counted." (We can thank the famous "theologian" Albert Einstein for that insightful quote.) Nevertheless, it's hard to deny that many churches exist primarily to keep their club members happy.

> *It's as if we've forgotten that the early church in the book of Acts existed primarily for those who were not already Christ-followers.*

Rick Warren, author of *The Purpose Driven Life*, is even more piercing: "The church that doesn't want to grow is saying to the world, 'You can go to hell.'" Disturbing, isn't it? Nevertheless, many churches continue to operate essentially as clubs, convinced they'd be letting God down if they closed up shop and sold their buildings.

Don't get me wrong; I care deeply about the church. The bride of Christ is the hope of the world. "Bride bashing" is not my thing. However, I also care deeply about the people God misses the most—those who need a safe space to ask their questions, share their doubts, voice their concerns, and even vent their anger toward God and the church. They need space to bring their real selves out into the light, to journey one step at a time toward the

cross. If not-yet-Christians are convinced the church is not a safe space to experience community or inquire about their spiritual yearnings, where *is* that space? And what does that look like in a world that increasingly says no to our traditional God Spaces?

START FROM THE HEART

If we're going to create God Space for others, it has to start inside *us*. It takes safe people to create safe places. First Corinthians 6:19 says that when we become Christians, our bodies are temples of the Holy Spirit. But Jesus did not send the Holy Spirit to simply *reside in* our bodies but to *preside over* them.

If we're going to create God Space for others, it has to start inside us. It takes safe people to create safe places.

Unfortunately, we're naturally predisposed toward resisting this holy takeover. *My* space, *my* desires, *my* needs, *my* money, *my* time—this "me, myself, and I" list of entitlements goes on forever. God wants to deliver us from this way of thinking. God Space begins where the natural gives way to the supernatural. We're urged, in Romans 12:1, to offer our bodies as living sacrifices. We can't create God Space until we've allowed God to create space in us first. The following story illustrates this truth.

MY AIRPLANE STORY

For 10 years, I served as ministry director for the Athletes in Action basketball team. During the fall, our team played college-basketball powerhouses like Duke, North Carolina, UCLA, Indiana, and Kentucky. At halftime or right after the game, our team was given the opportunity to share with the crowd how Christ had made a difference in our lives. Our travel schedule was usually horrendous, as we flew from city to city to play these schools before the regular season. Late nights and early mornings were all part of being on the road with AIA.

One particular season, our team played seven games in seven nights. After the sixth game, I was exhausted. The next morning we headed to the airport to catch a 6 o'clock flight. I waited until the very last minute to board so I could occupy a row with no one else in it, stretch out, and catch a nap

before we landed. I found several pillows, pulled down the window shade, stretched out, and began to enjoy the rest that my mind and body needed.

Just then I heard the flight attendant exhort a passenger to hurry because the plane was about to leave. The next thing I knew, the extrovert of all extroverts was asking for her seat on the aisle in the row I was trying to sleep in. I sat up and repositioned myself so she could sit down and I could go back to sleep. However, this was not what God had in mind.

Dianne introduced herself and asked me if I knew which basketball team was on board. I answered her as quickly as possible and lapsed back into a semi-comatose state. Dianne apparently did not have a grasp of the obvious, as she began to pepper me with questions about Athletes in Action. Her barrage of questions was stirring up a civil war within me. I prayed, "Please, God, I want to be off the clock for a while. I do not want to talk with this lady, let alone be your ambassador to her."

I don't know about you, but I never seem to wrestle with God and win. God wanted me to create space for him to work in this encounter. It's taken me a long time to truly understand what Jesus means when he tells us that we must lose daily if we are going to truly win (Luke 9:23). This death to self—*my* space—is where God Space begins to form. This is exactly what happened that day. I eventually gave in and allowed God to have his way in and through me. It didn't take long before the Holy Spirit began to guide me into Dianne's life.

I had no idea where the conversation would lead. After five minutes of everyday pleasantries, I learned that Dianne's passion was art. She excitedly shared her lifelong aspiration to move to Santa Fe and open her own art studio. I wondered aloud what was holding her back. She told me that her husband was not willing to leave Indianapolis, and I replied that it must be difficult to have the two loves of your life diametrically opposed to each other. Immediately she lowered her voice and said, "I've never told anyone this before, but I'm seriously considering leaving my husband and my son because I don't want this dream to go unfulfilled."

I asked for permission to share something I thought she might find helpful, and she granted it. I told Dianne that when I face major decisions, I like to play out the probabilities of where each decision might eventually lead. I asked her if she'd like to walk through this exercise, and she enthusiastically agreed. After five minutes, she came to the conclusion that choosing art

over family, or family over art, were both less than desirable. She said, "I feel like this is a no-win situation. What do you think I should do?"

Before I tell you what I told her, let's replay this scene, dissecting it as we go.

I boarded the plane consumed by my agenda. The Holy Spirit wrestled with me to let go and to be open to God's agenda for the duration of the flight. I eventually gave in. This death to self is *always* a prerequisite for creating God Space. Now that God had his way in me, he could also have his way in my conversation with Dianne. Spirit-led listening and wondering create safe places for people to bring their real selves into the light. When they do, they usually reveal a specific need that requires a divine solution.

Let's get back to the conversation. I responded to Dianne's question with the following "spiritual appetizer" (more on this in Chapter 8). I said, "When life's problems exceed my finite resources, I like to talk to someone with infinite resources. All I can tell you, Dianne, is that when I pray, 'coincidences' seem to happen."

Dianne immediately consumed my spiritual snack. Instantly the lights came on as she recalled a time in her life when she talked to God regularly. She said, "Those were the happiest days of my life." Dianne's heart immediately opened up, so I asked her if she'd be interested in looking at what the Bible has to say about seeking God for direction. Again, she was eager to hear. We spent the remainder of the flight using the Bible as the focal point for our "divine dialogue" (Chapter 9 develops that idea).

Have you ever stopped to wonder why these stories always seem to happen on airplanes? Every Christian speaker and leader I know seems to have an airplane story. I think it's because on an airplane, your spirituality has no bearing on where you sit or whom you sit next to. God uses this to bring Christians and non-Christians together as fellow sojourners heading in the same direction. Common ground, close proximity, no cell phones, and the belief that you will never again see the people you are sitting next to create greater possibilities for the natural and the supernatural to collide in meaningful ways.

SOMEONE ELSE'S AIRPLANE STORY

The following happened to a man I deeply respect because he creates God Space everywhere he goes. His name is Harvey, and here's his story—retold in my words, with my interjections—to highlight what he did to create God Space.

Harvey was on a flight to Zurich, Switzerland, and was seated next to a woman from India named Badhra. Early in the flight, he discovered that she was living and working in the U.S. as a doctor, and was traveling to Mumbai to visit family. As they continued to talk, Harvey asked Badhra if she was of the Hindu faith. She said, "No, I am a Jainist, which is similar."

Harvey responded, "That's very interesting. I have not heard about Jainism. Would you mind telling me about your faith?" *(The conversation had reached this point because Harvey had taken a sincere interest in what mattered most to Badhra.)*

As she described Jainism, Harvey asked clarifying questions to better understand her faith. *(Harvey entered the conversation in humility, as a listener and a learner, seeking to understand before seeking to be understood.)*

Toward the end of their conversation, Harvey said, "I have found that most faiths have some hope attached to them to motivate people's involvement. Tell me: What does the Jainist hope in?" *(Harvey continued to explore her worldview by raising sincere questions that he was wondering about.)*

She paused and then answered, "There is no hope in Jainism." *(Knowing he had about 10 hours with Badhra, Harvey chose to say nothing about Christianity. Yet. He wisely chose instead to prayerfully wait on the Lord. Badhra may have been expecting an agenda from Harvey, but as she continued to experience space to go at her own pace, she developed trust.)*

Shortly after this conversation, their meals came, and they casually chatted as they ate. Afterward, Harvey read for a while. Later, Badhra turned to him and asked, "Am I right in assuming that you are a Christian?"

Harvey replied, "Yes, I am."

"Oh, I have always wanted to know what it means to be a Christian. Would you mind telling me?"

Harvey did not hesitate to share the gospel with her. He wisely emphasized the hope that Christians have because of Jesus' claims. *(Harvey cued into the lack of hope Badhra described in Jainism.)* Badhra listened carefully, asked thoughtful questions, and thanked Harvey profusely when he'd finished.

Later on in the flight, Badhra began talking to the man on the other side of her, Akmed, who was from Iran. Suddenly she turned to Harvey and said, "I have just been talking to Akmed, and I think you would enjoy our conversation. Akmed is a Muslim, and I have told him that you are a Christian and

I am a Jainist. He would like to hear more about Christianity—would you mind telling him what you told me?"

Harvey said he would be happy to, but suggested there might be a better way. "How about if I listen while you tell Akmed what you heard me say, and I'll add or correct anything after you've finished? *(Harvey wisely asked Badhra to express what he had shared with her, so Badhra could internalize what she'd learned and deepen its impression upon her.)*

"Ah, very good," Badhra said, and seemed delighted as she shared with Akmed. "How did I do?" she asked afterward. Harvey assured her that she had presented the gospel perfectly. This led to a stimulating spiritual conversation that lasted for several hours. *(Harvey intentionally created room by creating a safe place for these two people to do what we are all taught not to do: talk about religion. He didn't make them go there; he created room for the possibility.)*

Though neither Badhra nor Akmed made a decision to become a Christian during the flight, Harvey was certain that they both now understood the gospel and the differences between Christianity and their own religions by the time they landed in Zurich. Now *that's* an airplane story!

Here's the million-dollar question: How do we *naturally* create room for spiritual conversations like that in our everyday lives? Surely God doesn't intend for us to wait until our next ride on an airplane!

The following chapters are intended to answer this question by giving you one piece of the puzzle at a time. I hope that by the time you've finished this book, your confidence and competence will be stretched to the point that you'll have your own stories to share.

So let's begin with a broad working definition of God Space.

DEFINING GOD SPACE

God Space is where...

...God is felt and encountered in tangible ways that address the longings and cries of the heart.

...we come to the end of our own finite resources and experience the infinite resources of God.

...the natural gives way to the supernatural.

...seeds of faith are planted, watered, and nurtured.

...gentleness and respect are present, judgment is absent, and divine dialogue flows naturally because trust has been established.

...the invisible principles of God's kingdom are made visible in ways people can see, touch, and feel.

...friends of sinners—in other words, *our* friends—dwell.

...the topic of God can be explored freely without agendas, biases, and personal convictions getting in the way.

...cynics, skeptics, scoffers, and spiritually curious people alike can raise their questions, share their doubts, voice their concerns, and even vent their anger toward God and the church.

...the "unworthy" feel safe enough to bring their real selves out into the light, and to journey, one step at a time, toward the magnetic pull they sense deep in their souls.

...spiritual curiosity is aroused, and the message of Christianity becomes plausible.

From INFORMATION to TRANSFORMATION

This book is meant to be experienced, not merely read. Therefore, each chapter concludes with practical assignments, so you can begin *having* those experiences. If you approach these ideas with a teachable heart, the definitions of God Space that you've just read will, more and more, become your reality.

Jesus was called many things during his short time here on earth. My favorite title for him is found in Matthew 11:19 and Luke 7:34 where Jesus acknowledges his awareness of the fact that many were calling him "a friend of sinners." In my mind, no title gets at the heart of why Jesus came to earth more than this one. It so closely coincides with his mission stated in Luke 19:10: "For the Son of Man came to seek and to save what was lost."

If we're going to make God's "invisible kingdom" become visible, then Christ's heart needs to be formed in us. Prayerfully ponder the following questions that reflect the essence of God Space. Grade yourself by using the following scale for each question. Jot down a number at the end of each question. When you have finished, add your numbers together to assess where you are in your journey.

1	2	3	4	5	6	7	8	9	10
NEVER				SOMETIMES					ALWAYS

1. Can you overlook un-Christlike attitudes and lifestyles in your efforts to connect with others?

2. Are you able to suspend your judgment for long periods of time around not-yet-Christians?

3. Do you consistently seek to understand the not-yet-Christians you know before seeking to be understood by them?

4. Are you patient enough to wait for the not-yet-Christians in your life to ask for your opinion?

5. Be honest: Do you *like* people who are far from God?

6. Do people who are far from God like *you*? For example: Are you invited to "party-parties"?

7. Does your body language communicate an open-hearted acceptance of the not-yet-Christians in your life?

8. Are you able to communicate acceptance to not-yet-Christians without endorsing their lifestyles?

9. In your relationships with not-yet-Christians, do you typically offer kindness rather than "rightness"?

10. Is your heart consistently broken and filled with compassion for the not-yet-Christians in your life?

---

85 to 100—Congratulations! You might be frequently misunderstood by Christians, but the not-yet-Christians in your life are undoubtedly drawn toward the heart of Jesus formed in you. Keeping walking in this light.

65 to 85—You must decrease, and Jesus must increase—one heart attitude at a time. Embrace the people and the situations in your life as God attempts to prune those heart attitudes that are not bearing fruit for his kingdom.

Under 65—Jesus needs to do something *in* you before he can do something *through* you. Consider spending less time doing religious activities, and more time asking God to do the soul surgery needed to form the heart of Jesus in you.

CHAPTER 2
Spiritual Conversation-Killers

In April 2003, National Public Radio aired a story about a standoff in Najaf, Iraq, between an angry mob of Shiites and a heavily armored patrol from the American 101st Airborne Division. Fearing that the soldiers were preparing to desecrate their holy shrine, hundreds of unarmed civilians pressed in toward the soldiers, waving their hands and shouting defiantly. Although the patrol's intentions were peaceful, the standoff would probably have been disastrous if not for the quick thinking of U.S. Lieutenant Colonel Christopher Hughes.

Hughes, who was in command that day, picked up a loudspeaker and barked out three simple commands to his troops. First, he told them to "take a knee"; second, to point their weapons toward the ground; and finally, to look up and give everyone in the hostile crowd a friendly smile. Astoundingly, in a few moments after they obeyed his order, the troops saw the demeanor of the crowd change. Hostility and defiance melted away, as smiles and friendly pats on the back replaced shaking fists and screaming voices.

Though it may not be immediately apparent, this story has important implications for spiritual conversations in a world that is becoming increasingly hostile to the traditional kinds of conversations Christians attempt to have. As author Ravi Zacharias says, "We must learn to find the back door to people's hearts because the front door is heavily guarded." Much like the Shiites that Lieutenant Colonel Hughes dealt with, many people we hope to reach for Jesus react defensively. They anticipate, and are amply prepared for, any direct attack on the holy places and sacred shrines of their hearts.

Our message rarely gets through because what they hear is "My worldview is better than your worldview, so let me tell you why I'm right and you're wrong." Instead of opening hearts to Jesus, many times we merely perpetuate the "us versus them" standoff. So how do we keep from becoming entangled in these no-win, never-ending quagmires?

a
SCRIPTURE
to meditate
on

The Message version of Colossians 4:5-6 puts the answer this way: "Use your heads as you live and work among outsiders. Don't miss a trick. Make the most of every opportunity. Be gracious in your speech. The goal is to bring out the best in others in a conversation, not put them down, not cut them out."

The first sentence of this passage perfectly describes Lt. Col. Hughes' approach that day in Najaf. He was *wise* in the way he related to people whose feelings and beliefs were so different from his. We must be equally wise if we want the quality and quantity of our spiritual conversations to increase. If you truly believe, as I do, that real wisdom comes from God, I encourage you to pause and invite the Holy Spirit to grant you this kind of wisdom as you read this book.

a
PRAYER
to offer

"God, open my eyes to the ways I may be hindering opportunities for spiritual conversations in my daily life."

I've found that God usually wants to do something *in* us before he can do something *through* us. He wants us to be transformed into the very message we are trying to share with others. That's why I strongly encourage you to do all the homework assignments in this chapter; if you don't, the rest of this book could be a wasted read. Identifying and eliminating the spiritual conversation-killers in your life is a pivotal part of each Christ-follower's journey toward internalizing the truth of Colossians 4:5-6.

Allow the Holy Spirit to have his way in your heart as you reflect on my top-10 list of spiritual conversation-killers. I'm all too familiar with each one of them. You see, I *failed* my way into writing this chapter, one spiritual conversation-killer at a time. So by all means, learn from my failures so you can avoid my mistakes.

Killer 1: AN UNBELIEVING HEART

After speaking with countless Christ-followers all over the world, I'm convinced that the number-one killer of spiritual conversation is unbelief. Please stop and prayerfully consider a question that penetrates to the heart of this conviction: *Do you really believe the people in your Monday-through-*

Saturday world want to talk about spiritual things? If you don't, I urge you to stop reading right now and invite Christ to help you with your unbelieving heart. Nothing else in this book will help you until you change your mind about this matter.

In Matthew 12:34b, Jesus tells us that our words reflect our hearts. I have found that we will miss opportunity after opportunity if we've decided that the people who cross our paths have no interest in talking about spiritual matters. For those of you who are skeptical of my assertion due to the spiritual climate of your geographic location, please give me the benefit of the doubt. I've had spiritual conversations with people all over the world, including the supposed "tough places." I think it's because the Holy Spirit has given me a conviction that if God has put eternity in every person's heart, which is what Ecclesiastes 3:11 tells us, then *all* people were made for spiritual conversations.

As I've learned how to naturally create God Space and avoid the next nine spiritual conversation-killers you will read about, spiritual conversations have become the norm, not the exception. Thomas Jefferson said that "when the heart is right, the feet are swift." Jesus said, "Everything is possible for him who believes" (Mark 9:23b). Your heart is the heart of the matter! Unbelief hampers the Holy Spirit's ability to advance God's kingdom through you, one spiritual conversation at a time.

Killer 2: PRE-CONVERSATION HISTORY

The second greatest deterrent to spiritual conversations occurs before most conversations even get started. In his book *UnChristian*, David Kinnaman quotes one outsider who described Christians this way: "Most people I meet assume that *Christian* means very conservative, entrenched in their thinking, anti-gay, anti-choice, angry, violent, illogical, empire builders; they want to convert everyone, and they generally cannot live peacefully with anyone who doesn't believe what they believe." Like it or not, our Christian jewelry, T-shirts, TV programs, tracts, and bumper stickers all serve to create a pre-conversation history that colors the perception of everyone we meet. This greatly inhibits the possibility of having spiritual conversations. When you identify with Jesus, you automatically inherit all the perceptions created by his followers. Getting out of this "Christian box" as quickly as possible is essential if you're going to have real conversations.

This became quite clear to me on a trip to Columbus, Ohio. I was speaking at the annual Summer Institute at Xenos, a church that is trying to live out many of the principles of this book. I was having a problem with one of the digital slides in my keynote presentation, so I went to the nearby computer store for help. The young lady assigned to work with me liked the challenging problem I presented to her. As she attempted to fix it, she was exposed to most of the content of my presentation. I sensed tension as she asked me to scroll through the clips and slides. At that moment, I realized that I wasn't just *in* the box—to her, I *was* the box.

Fortunately, the Holy Spirit helped get me out of the box with the following question: "I'm wondering if you would be willing to help me in another way. I'm here in town to speak to a large gathering of Christians who would like to learn how to talk to their friends about spiritual matters. Has anyone ever tried to do that with you?" She immediately ranted about her negative experiences with her Christian sister. As I began to reflectively listen to her, she began to calm down a little.

I asked, "If your sister were in the audience tomorrow, what would you like me to tell her so that your future conversations turn out a little better?" With that question, I had climbed out of the box. She began to realize that I was not like her sister. Now that her history was out on the table, I was able to move forward and avoid the landmines that might blow up our discussion about spiritual matters.

I left, wishing there *were* a way her sister could be in my audience the next day. Of course, that didn't happen. I decided to share this story in the hope that someday she'll read this book and connect the dots. Whether she does or not, this experience helped me see that we can't ignore people's pre-conversation histories if we hope to increase the quality and quantity of our spiritual conversations.

This leads us to a far more personal question: What if *you're* the one who's contributed to someone's negative perception of Christianity? This question cuts deep into the core of all our relationships, and Jesus may have had it in mind when he said that we "will have to give account on the day of judgment for every careless word [we] have spoken" (Matthew 12:36).

Careless words erode our credibility. Have you ever found yourself wanting to talk to somebody about spiritual things, but didn't because you were afraid the word *hypocrite* might be thrown in your direction? I'm convinced that, next to unbelief, this fear muzzles more Christians than any other factor.

This was made apparent to me one day while I was sharing some of these

thoughts with a group of women who met regularly in a neighborhood Bible study. Carol explained that she frequently spent time with a group of non-Christian women. Every time they got together, these women bashed their husbands. Carol had the courage to admit to me that all too often, she joined right in. How could she now turn around and talk about God's design for marriage, or anything else concerning Christianity, without inviting scathing comments?

Only God knows how many of us might be two confessions away

from the most significant spiritual conversations of our lives.

Have you been there and done that? I have, and I know only one way to rectify the situation. It starts and ends with confession. Start with God by agreeing with him that the things you said did not reflect positively on him. Then humble yourself before those you said them to, and let those people know you were wrong to say the things you did. And rest assured: When you own your mistakes and call them what they are, spiritual conversations come. Only God knows how many of us might be two confessions away from the most significant spiritual conversations of our lives. (You'll discover more about how to rebuild burned bridges in Chapter 10.)

Killer 3: AWKWARD TRANSITIONS

Several years ago, I found myself at home alone on a Sunday afternoon, immersed in the last two minutes of a football game that would decide which team would go to the playoffs. I was annoyed when the doorbell rang. I prepared to stiff-arm (in Christian love, of course) whoever was at the door so I could get back to my football fix. When I opened the door, two Mormons stood ready to engage me in spiritual conversation.

I found myself suspended in a time warp, as they fumbled the ball early and often in their struggle to start a conversation with me. As I listened to their awkward attempts, images of bygone days flashed through my mind. I remembered times when I was the one trying to start such conversations, and I was filled with compassion for these two Mormons as I recalled stammering through awkward transitions I had memorized early on as a Christ-follower.

Awkward transitions create awkward feelings, which leave people feeling pretty uptight. Most of the people I know don't regularly sign up for conversations that leave them feeling weirded out.

This raises a question I'm asked quite often: "How do you transition into a spiritual conversation?" As I've probed to better understand this question, I've discovered that most Christ-followers are looking for a sure-fire transitional statement they can memorize that will produce great spiritual conversations every time they use it.

Maybe we should take a cue from Jesus on this one. If he didn't approach spiritual conversations this way, why should we?

I'm quite familiar with the transitions Christian workers are taught to use. Even when practiced and delivered flawlessly, these transitions tend to create awkward feelings when people realize you're trying to take the conversation somewhere. If their hearts aren't prepared to go there, it might be the last spiritual conversation you'll ever have with them. In Chapter 7, I'll discuss how we can avoid awkward transitions and move naturally into spiritual conversations.

Killer 4: OUR LANGUAGE, NOT THEIRS

While I'm on the subject of Mormons, I have to share a funny story that I hope will make Killer 4 seem quite obvious. A few years ago, my brother's job required him to move to Salt Lake City. After the family had settled into the neighborhood, one of the neighbors came over to welcome them. As this woman began to engage my sister-in-law in conversation, she asked, "Are you LDS [Latter-Day Saints]?" My sister-in-law looked at my brother and replied, "Well, neither one of us is ADD [Attention Deficit Disorder], so we probably aren't LDS either."

I still laugh when I recall this story. However, when I think about its implications for spiritual conversations, I'm quite sobered. When we lead with questions such as "Are you saved?" or "Have you been born again?" people feel like outsiders. When we speak "Christianese," we are unwittingly saying, "If you want to have a spiritual conversation with me, you'll have to do so on my terms."

Jesus modeled something quite different. He used the language of the day to speak of heavenly truths. The Apostle Paul asked believers to pray that he would proclaim the message clearly (Colossians 4:4). When we use our language rather than theirs, we confuse people and often leave them feeling confused or stupid. Jesus used language that built bridges and opened doors. We can do the same by learning to translate spiritual truth into the everyday vernacular of the people we converse with.

Killer 5: DISRESPECT

Sometimes I think my "spiritual gift" is being quick to speak and slow to listen. James 1:19 tells us to do the opposite. If we aren't quick to listen and slow to speak, it will be quite easy for others to feel disrespected.

There are lots of other ways to unknowingly demonstrate disrespect in our conversations. Being condescending or "parental" will do it every time. When we exceed the speed limit, run the stop signs, or hijack the conversation (the three most common "evangelistic misdemeanors," which I'll describe in detail in Chapter 5), we are not treating others the way we would like to be treated. Personally, I don't regularly show up for conversations in which I know I'm going to be disrespected.

Killer 6: AGENDAS

In the movie *The Big Kahuna*, Larry asks Bob (an evangelical Christian) how he ended up talking to Dick Fuller (a prospective business client) about religion. As Larry continues to probe, Bob eventually admits that the conversation got started due to a question he asked to steer the conversation toward spiritual matters. Larry astutely observes that Bob was looking for the opportunity to talk about what he believed. He goes on to say, "The conversation was not allowed to have a natural course because somebody was at the helm directing it."

◄ a MOVIE to watch

Later in the movie, Phil—another salesman—pulls Bob aside and shares this advice with him: "If you want to talk to somebody honestly, as a human being, ask him about his kids, find out what his dreams are—just to find out, for no other reason. Because as soon as you lay your hands on a conversation to steer it, it's not a conversation anymore; it's a pitch. And you're not a human being; you're a marketing rep."

After watching this movie, I realized that Larry and Phil had some advice for me as well as Bob. During my early years in ministry, I became known as one of the chief marketing reps for Jesus. Unfortunately, I was actually affirmed for steering conversations toward my sales pitch for Jesus. *Spiritual conversations should be our ultimate motive, not our ulterior motive.*

◄ a QUOTE to memorize

If people are ready for the agenda you have in mind for the conversation, you'll be warmly embraced. If they aren't, you'll be assigned a label that will kill most of your opportunities for spiritual conversations in the future.

Killer 7: CONTROL

How long does it usually take for you to seize a conversation and dominate it with your worldview? This is a question I wish someone had challenged me to think about early in my spiritual journey. During the 1980s, I started the Athletes in Action ministry at the University of Tennessee. If you had dropped in on one of my appointments with an athlete back then, this is what you probably would have seen: I'd usually begin by asking a couple of questions to break the ice. I rarely listened to the answers because I didn't want to detour from the destination I had planned for the conversation. After I broke the ice, I usually asked a question I had memorized to turn the conversation toward spiritual things. I spent the rest of the hour sharing something I believed the other person needed to hear. From beginning to end, I was in control of the conversation.

How long does it usually take for you to seize a conversation and dominate it with your worldview?

Other ministries are even more extreme. They teach their workers to treat questions as smokescreens. Each question is deflected so the Christian worker can get back to his or her scripted presentation. Is it any wonder more and more people are saying "no thanks" to these conversations? If you want to have a meaningful spiritual conversation, you'll need to give up the idea of controlling it.

I'm convinced that many Christ-followers are afraid to be in settings where they're not in control of the conversation. This is why churches and ministries die. When we insist on having conversations where only our fans are present, only when we choose to, and only during activities we're comfortable with, we might as well start digging a 6-foot hole and playing taps. It's only a matter of time before a church or ministry that insists on playing only "home games" begins to fade into oblivion.

Jesus told his disciples not to worry about what to say or how to say it because the Holy Spirit would give them what they needed when they needed it (Matthew 10:19-20). There's nothing packaged or scripted about that—just an admonition to submit to the Holy Spirit's guidance, and the promise that the Spirit will be there when we do.

Recently, as I was leaving a social gathering attended by very few churchgoers, I overheard a pastor say, "If you'd like to talk again sometime,

you know where to find me on Sunday mornings." I'm not sure what the pastor intended by this parting comment, but I thought about how different the outcome might be if the pastor was as willing to play as many road games as he was home games.

Killer 8: JUDGMENT

To many people in our culture, Christians are considered the "disagreement people." We've worked hard to earn this label, one reaction at a time. Our body language, tone of voice, and verbal responses are dead giveaways to the reality that we disagree with much of what people in our culture are saying and doing. When we become self-designated spiritual umpires, calling balls and strikes on the culture by writing letters to the editor, calling in to talk radio shows, and staging boycotts of one kind or another, our reactions speak for themselves.

Essentially, we are sending the culture this message: Not only do we not endorse your *point of view*, we also don't accept *you*. This lack of acceptance crushes opportunities for spiritual conversations. *Acceptance* does not mean *endorsement*. When we confuse the two, we destroy the very space God wants to work in.

Many times, not-yet-Christians will say or do things just to see how we'll react. This is often a test to determine whether it's safe enough for them to engage with us in real conversations. Reacting to things we hear or see comes naturally for most of us. But what we need are *supernatural* responses—"love, joy, peace, patience, kindness, goodness, faithfulness, gentleness and self-control" (Galatians 5:22-23)—that communicate radical acceptance, if we hope to create space for spiritual conversations to happen naturally.

> Acceptance *does not mean* endorsement. *When we confuse the two, we destroy the very space God wants to work in.*

Killer 9: COMBATIVENESS

It's exhilarating to watch two good tennis players volley back and forth. Each tries to cause the other to get out of position in order to hit a decisive shot—a winner—and score a point. Unfortunately, I used to view spiritual conversations in the same way. I viewed the person I was talking with as my opponent who must be won to my Christian point of view.

I interned with Josh McDowell. I was trained by the best when it comes to apologetics. On many occasions, I started my conversations with an overpowering serve. I then prepared myself to pepper winners at my opponent, who in many cases had walked away from the conversation the moment the contest began.

Even if my opponent was up for it, most of the time these worldview challenges led to heated debates, and heated debates eventually gave way to arguments. In the end, I never argued anyone into the kingdom of God. As I once heard Dallas Willard say, "It's very difficult to be right about something without hurting someone with it." We need to remember that not-yet-Christians are not the enemy; they're *victims of* the enemy. We're called to move into culture with compassion and check our "onward, Christian soldiers" mind-sets at the door.

Killer 10: "IT'S ALL ABOUT ME"

Have you ever been in a conversation in which you felt you couldn't get a word in edgewise, or the spotlight never seemed to shift off the person who was talking? If so, I bet you just can't wait for your next conversation with that person!

We need to remember that not-yet-Christians are not the enemy; they're victims of the enemy. We are called to move into culture with compassion and check our "onward, Christian soldiers" mind-sets at the door.

I believe that Christians can slip into these "it's all about me" kinds of conversations naturally. Because we're convinced we have the absolute truth, we believe that what we think is all that really matters. This kind of thinking quickly turns conversations into monologues in which we end up talking to ourselves. We need to realize that if people aren't asking us what we believe, we might be wiser to keep the spotlight on what *they* believe and think. The secret to *being interesting* in a conversation is to *be interested.* Philippians 2:4 encourages us to "look not only to [our] own interests, but also to the interests of others."

At the end of the day, I want people to follow Jesus. I want to keep the spotlight on him and what he said, not on what I personally think or believe.

This requires me to bring the Bible into conversations. We'll get into this more in Chapter 9.

BEGIN AGAIN

Just one of these conversation-killers can close down your opportunities for spiritual conversation in a relationship for a lifetime. The good news is that failure is usually never fatal or final; it's just an opportunity to begin again more intelligently. Chapter 10 will give you some practical ideas for reclaiming missed opportunities. I urge you to take these ideas seriously, and to prayerfully consider how to implement them.

Lieutenant Colonel Hughes saved the day when he acted wisely toward people whose values were different from his. Let's follow his example. Let's "take a knee" (a position of humility, from which we approach conversations as listeners and learners); let's point our guns to the ground (back away from confrontational attempts to overpower people with dogmatic certainties that leave others defensive and convinced of our arrogance); let's look up and smile (communicate that we are respectful, warm, friendly, and caring people).

I wonder what would happen if we were willing to let go of the attitudes and practices that kill the potential for spiritual conversations. I'd like to think that Lt. Col. Hughes would recommend the rest of this book as a field manual for a different kind of Christian soldier for today's world.

From **INFORMATION** to **TRANSFORMATION**

UnChristian by David Kinnaman and Gabe Lyons (Baker Books, 2007)

a
BOOK
to read

As you read through the top-10 list of spiritual conversation-killers, what did the Holy Spirit bring to mind? What might be impeding the quality and quantity of spiritual conversations in your life?

a
QUESTION
to answer

Ask the not-yet-Christians in your life to describe what they experience when conversations turn to spiritual matters. Seek to understand their feelings by probing into what prompts them to feel that way.

a
**FAITH
EXPERIMENT**
to try

CHAPTER 3

Noticing Your Way Into Spiritual Conversations

After our last chapter, you might be feeling as if you climbed in the ring with Rocky Balboa. It's never fun to have our failures pointed out. Nevertheless, I hope you caught the true spirit of the chapter. We'll always be who we've always been if we always do what we've always done. So let's move past what doesn't work and start focusing on what *does*.

If we're going to focus on what works, we need to make sure we're seeing the world around us clearly.

In 1862, Dutch ophthalmologist Herman Snellen discovered a direct correlation between the sizes of letters viewed from certain distances and the quality of one's eyesight. The Snellen test is administered by covering one eye and reading aloud letters on a chart. When you finish the test, you're given two numbers that describe your ability to see images from a certain distance. The first number represents the distance between you and the chart. The second number represents your ability to recognize the letters on a particular line of the chart. Normal eyesight is designated 20/20. If you have 20/40 vision, this means that from 20 feet away you're only able to identify images on a line that a person with normal vision could identify from 40 feet away. You're considered legally blind if you have 20/200 vision, because you can only recognize detail at 20 feet that a person with normal vision would recognize from 200 feet away.

We'll always be who we've always been

if we always do what we've always done.

Wouldn't it be interesting if someone developed a similar test to help us determine the quality of our spiritual vision? How do you think you'd score on a test like that? What would it be like to have 20/20 spiritual vision? I'm wondering how many of us would be declared spiritually blind. Only God knows!

IMPROVING YOUR VISION

I've found a direct correlation between how I view my world and what I'm moved to do. When I start seeing the world the way Jesus does, I'm moved to do something about it in his name. In Luke 11:34, Jesus says, "Your eye is the lamp of your body. When your eyes are good, your whole body also is full of light. But when they are bad, your body also is full of darkness."

a

SCRIPTURE ◀

to ponder

Paul understood this correlation. In Ephesians 1:18 he prays for the "eyes of the heart" to be enlightened. The Bible makes it clear that one's eyesight has everything to do with one's insight. Insight is gained one revelation at a time, by allowing the light of God's Word to penetrate the darkness of our hearts. When we do, the fog begins to lift, and our spiritual vision is sharpened. We now have God's bigger picture to guide us.

How we see others in our world is a strong indicator of whether we have 20/20 spiritual vision. Matthew 9:36 gives us a snapshot of keen spiritual vision. "When he saw the crowds, he had compassion on them, because they were harassed and helpless, like sheep without a shepherd." We'll never see the world with the same degree of spiritual vision that Jesus did. Fortunately, Jesus gave us some pretty good indicators of what it looks like to have 20/20 spiritual vision.

For example, Jesus said, "Blessed are the pure in heart, for they will see God" (Matthew 5:8). Jesus not only promised this, but Hebrews 10:22 assures us that we can experience this verse personally because of what Jesus did on the cross for us. Jesus removed our "cataracts" and made it possible for us to see with spiritual eyes. Isn't that what we all affirm whenever we sing "Amazing Grace"—"I once was...blind, but now I see"?

Because we have spiritual eyes, we are able to properly view eternity.

We no longer need to be fooled by the mirage of fame, wealth, power, and self-righteousness. Jesus said, "Anyone who believes in God's Son has eternal life. Anyone who doesn't obey the Son will never experience eternal life but remains under God's angry judgment" (John 3:36, New Living Translation). At the foot of the cross, the playing field is level. As 2 Corinthians 5:16 reminds us, we are no longer to see others "from a worldly point of view." Maybe this would help us to have more compassion on those who appear to have everything in the world's eyes, but are spiritually bankrupt in God's.

LEARNING TO NOTICE

Jesus also tells us, in blunt, uncompromising language how to improve our spiritual vision: "Hypocrite! First get rid of the log in your own eye; then you will see well enough to deal with the speck in your friend's eye" (Matthew 7:5, NLT). Ouch! Our ability to clearly see the world around us is directly related to how many logs we've removed—or haven't removed—from our own eyes.

an
EXPERIMENT
to try

Here's another way to determine if you're ready to notice your way into spiritual conversations. Please put this book down and jump on the Internet. Go to YouTube.com and do a search for awareness tests. The one you're looking for is called "Test Your Awareness: Do The Test" and starts off with a man saying, "This is an awareness test. How many passes does the team in white make?" Everyone in the clip then takes turns passing basketballs around.

Did you get the right answer? Did you see the _____? If you watched the clip, you can fill in the blank. If you didn't, please go do it now. You're on the honor system here. This is one of your assignments to help you apply what you're reading from this chapter. Here's the point of the whole clip: *"It's easy to miss something you're not really looking for."* Haven't you found that to be true?

I think this is the big idea in the story of the good Samaritan (Luke 10:30-37). The first two men passed by the injured man because they were intentionally blind to his suffering. They didn't want to see people the way Jesus saw them. The good Samaritan, however, had 20/20 spiritual vision. His eyes were connected to his heart. As a result, when he noticed the man by the side of the road, he was moved by compassion.

JESUS GLASSES

If it truly is easy to miss something we're not really looking for, then maybe we need to increase our awareness. Maybe we need "Jesus glasses," the kind that allow us to see the world around us the way Jesus does. When we start to notice others with our Jesus glasses on, something happens inside us. Like a defibrillator, the Holy Spirit stimulates the heart of Jesus to beat in us. His compassion melts away the coldness in our hearts. Our callousness toward others is replaced with a genuine concern. What does this look like in this day and age? I'm glad you asked.

Once again, I'd like you to put this book down and get on the **an EXPERIMENT to try** Internet. This time go to SermonSpice.com. Do a search for the clip entitled "Get Service," which features a young man who is given glasses that allow him to see the real needs of those around him. As you watch the clip, turn this question over a few times in your mind: When was the last time you saw someone in your world in this way? Having insight like this is one indication that we are seeing our world with 20/20 spiritual vision.

God gives us tests like the ones in the video every day.

> **When we start to notice others with our Jesus glasses on, something happens inside us...His compassion melts away the coldness in our hearts. Our callousness toward others is replaced with a genuine concern.**

If we aren't careful, the busyness of life will lead to intentional blindness, and we'll fail these tests day after day. I have a name for this inwardly focused, nearsighted kind of life. I call it "*my*-opia." The best way I know to curb this disease, which clouds our spiritual vision, is to start every **a PRAYER to offer** morning with this simple prayer: "Lord Jesus, as I interact with others today, help me to see them as you do."

An outwardly focused mindset causes us to start listening with our eyes, seeing with our ears, and responding with our hearts. (If you watched the clip, you'll understand that sentence.) And it sends others a powerful message: "I notice you! You matter to me! You matter to God!" Noticing creates God Space in our relational encounters.

NOTICING LEADS TO CARING

Jim Henderson, founder of Doable Evangelism, is my official champion of the ministry of noticing. He sends people out to do noticing exercises. His instructions are simple: Go and notice others; then come back and share what you saw that maybe you hadn't noticed before. Jim is convinced, and so am I, that noticing is a prerequisite to caring about others and serving them in tangible ways that smuggle the gospel into their hearts.

Not only does noticing cause us to care for others, but it builds natural bridges to spiritual conversations. The Apostle Paul modeled this for us when he said, "Men of Athens! I *see* that in every way you are very religious. For as I walked around and *looked carefully* at your objects of worship..." (Acts 17:22b-23a, italics mine). If you want the rest of the story, finish reading Acts 17, but the point I want to make is that Paul essentially noticed his way into a spiritual conversation.

The simple act of noticing enables us to connect with others in authentic ways that pave the way for spiritual conversations to happen naturally. Instead of walking around with our periscopes down, the eyes of our hearts are turned outward to fully observe the world around us. The next story illustrates what following Paul's example looks like in the 21st century.

STOP PRAYING AND START NOTICING

I've had eight knee surgeries, so I've been forced to give up most of the competitive sports I enjoyed in my younger days. Now I just swim laps for the sake of my knee and my cardiovascular fitness. Whenever I'm out of town, I head for the nearest YMCA. One morning, I noticed that the lifeguard on duty was staring off into space. Lap after lap, I continued to notice that she didn't seem very happy. I usually pray while I swim, but on this day it was time to stop praying and start noticing. I finally stopped and said, "It seems like you're really bummed out about something. Is everything OK?"

She acknowledged that she was having some personal struggles. I listened to her for a while and then reflected back to her what I was hearing. After sensing that I understood, she became even more transparent. I listened! I wondered! I cared! I eventually asked her for permission to share a God thought with her that I hoped would help her in her struggles.

Noticing had opened the door for this to happen. She thanked me on numerous occasions for taking the time to care. *Care* is the word she chose,

but I think noticing came first. The caring came after my heart was touched by her pensiveness.

You might think I'm splitting hairs, but I want to make an important distinction here. If I had waited for my feelings to propel me into action that day, I would never have stopped swimming. The truth is, I don't naturally care about people I don't know.

Noticing requires me to respond, first, to what the Holy Spirit has allowed me to see. In obedience, I move toward people whether I *feel* like it or not. They might be strangers to me, but they are not strangers to God. Most of the time, I find God gives me his heart for people on the spot and in the moment. The caring comes after I've taken the initiative to show up with my Jesus glasses on. If I wait for feelings to come first, I'll miss the God Space he wants to create in and through me simply by noticing.

NOTICE—PRAY—AND REPEAT

The following story, submitted to the Doable Evangelism website, further illustrates this point.

> I work at a local community college and often buy lunch in the cafeteria. When I first encountered the lunch lady, she was taking my money. I noticed that she had short, gray hair and the kind of fingernail polish that changes according to holiday. I also noticed that her nametag said "Dottie."
>
> The next week I told her I liked her nails, and I noticed that she had a bad chest cold. I prayed for her health, but I didn't mention my prayer to her.
>
> The following week I asked how her cold was. She said it wasn't getting better and she was worried because she is a breast cancer survivor. She was afraid that the cancer might have come back.
>
> It was two more weeks before I saw Miss Dottie again. When I asked how she was, she said that the doctors had told her the cancer was back! We teared up together, and I promised to pray for her.
>
> The next week I brought Miss Dottie a present. It was a book called *Thanks for the Mammogram!* It is a book on facing cancer with faith, hope, and humor. I also gave her a card thanking her for always being there to smile

at me, and I offered to go to treatment with her sometime. She grabbed my hand and said, "Thank you so much!" Then she asked me to come around to the other side of the booth to give her a hug.

Later Miss Dottie had to quit her job due to her cancer. Our faith community hosted a "We love Miss Dottie" fundraiser and raised over $1,000 for her family. She was astonished that strangers would care for her in this way.

I'm grateful to God that I noticed Miss Dottie. God has planted her firmly in my heart, and I can't stop praying for her.

Jim Henderson posted his take on why this story offers so much hope for ordinary Christians. This young lady noticed someone she had *seen* many times before. She made a few mental notes about the woman who took her money at the lunch counter. She did nothing bold or dramatic, but the simple act of noticing connected her to Dottie in a new way. The next time she saw her, she prayed for her covertly. This connected her in a deeper way.

The next time she saw her, she asked, "How are you?" and then just listened. The conversation deepened when Miss Dottie shared her concern about cancer.

These are all ordinary things. Anyone could do this much, but most people don't. This young lady fell in love with Miss Dottie and ended up caring about her so much that she offered to go to treatments with her and raise money on her behalf. Her final line says it all for me: "God has planted her firmly in my heart, and I can't stop praying for her."

Noticing others will change your life. It will plant people firmly in your heart. When that happens, everything changes—including you.

NOTICING, YET NOT NOTICING

I think this is a concept better caught than taught. Before I close this chapter, I'd like to share one more story that has served as a form of "Lasik surgery" to help people regain their spiritual vision.

Ironically, this story is about a man who had a *huge* passion for noticing—butterflies. He traveled the world to add rare and unusual species to his collection. As he moved toward retirement, there was only one butterfly left in the world that he needed to make his collection complete. This rare

butterfly had only been spotted a few times in the deserts of Utah. So he made arrangements to stay with some friends who lived near the desert.

Day after day, he got up early and came home late, driven by his desire to net this elusive butterfly. Day after day, he returned empty-handed. Near the end of the first month, he thought he saw the prized butterfly floating around in the dry desert breeze. His heart began to pound, as he knew this might be his only opportunity to net the rare butterfly. The sun was beginning to go down, so he had to move fast. As he raced to the area where he had spotted the butterfly, he heard what sounded like a man groaning in distress. He quickly tried to block it out of his mind because he didn't want to miss his opportunity to capture the prize of a lifetime.

As he moved toward the butterfly, he made a quick decision to investigate the groaning noise after he had netted the butterfly. He pulled out his special gear, and within a couple of minutes, he had managed to net his dream. Euphoria swept over him. His quest to posses the world's greatest butterfly collection had been realized!

In his excitement, he forgot about the sounds he had heard just a few minutes earlier. He headed home to show his friends the butterfly that very few people in the whole world had ever seen. As he recounted his story, he suddenly was jarred by the reality that he had forgotten to investigate the sounds he had heard earlier.

He and his friends got up before dawn the next morning and made their way back to where he thought he had heard the sounds. After looking around for about an hour, they came across the body of an old prospector. Some time during the night, when the temperature in the desert had plummeted, the old man had passed away.

Chasing butterflies has consequences, doesn't it? We are what we cherish. What we cherish most, we notice most.

From **INFORMATION** *to* **TRANSFORMATION**

The following exercises are intended to help you put on Jesus glasses. When Christians begin to see people the way Jesus sees them, the Holy Spirit produces the love and compassion that make reaching out to others irresistible.

a
FAITH EXPERIMENT ▶
to try

With other Christian friends, go to places where Christians are usually absent and not-yet-Christians are present in full force: bars, rock concerts, parties, happy hours, and so on. Prayerfully consider what you see and hear. Gather with your friends afterward, and share what you noticed, what you felt, what disturbed you, what you felt God was showing you. Talk about what you learned—and how to respond to it—as a community.

a
FAITH EXPERIMENT ▶
to try

The next time you go to a restaurant, find out your server's name. When he or she brings your food, thank the person, and explain that it's your custom to thank God for every meal. Look the person in the eye, use his or her name, and ask if there is currently anything going on in the person's life that you could pray for when you thank God for your food. Listen, observe body language, and proceed as the Spirit leads. Regardless of what happens, leave a generous tip!

a
FAITH EXPERIMENT ▶
to try

For the next 31 days, begin each morning with the following prayer: "Lord Jesus, as I interact with others today, help me to see them as you do." Each day, keep a written record or journal of things you hadn't noticed before. Ask God what he'd like you to do with what you're noticing.

a
WEBSITE ▶
to
check out

doableevangelism.com

CHAPTER 4

Serving Your Way Into Spiritual Conversations

B ack in the early '80s, I traveled to the Philippines with Sports Ambassadors, the sports ministry of Overseas Crusades. We were a team of college basketball players from around the country who used our love of sport to share our love for God. We played two to three games every day in the basketball-crazed culture of the Philippines.

The Filipino kids acted as if we were NBA stars. Everywhere we went, they lined up for autographs. They were also fascinated by the hair on our bodies (I was told the men in their culture don't usually have much body hair). Game after game, kids would stroke the hair on my sweaty legs or pull at the hair under my arms while I was on the bench. It was strange to have kids invading my personal space in this way.

The kids were one thing, but the older Filipino men pushed me over the top. After the game, they insisted on holding my hand in public while we walked and talked. This was *way* out of my comfort zone! Fortunately, the full-time missionaries there helped me realize that every culture has different boundaries when it comes to personal space. Otherwise, I might have been put in jail for knocking some Filipino man out when he insisted on this public display of affection!

Since then, I've traveled all over the world on missionary endeavors. Each culture I've visited has its own comfort zone when it comes to personal space. Ignoring these social norms can set you up for some awkward relational moments.

This also holds true when we insensitively enter someone's "spiritual comfort zone." A person who is flooded with uncomfortable feelings cannot decipher good intentions very well. This might explain why so many non-Christians distrust even well-intentioned Christians. Maybe they feel as I did in the Philippines, or as I did one weekend awhile back when I was helping my dad on our family farm.

My dad asked me if I had some time to make a hay delivery with him. After we had finished unloading the hay, he sent me in to get a check for the delivery. As I walked in the door, I encountered a man sitting in a recliner with his injured leg propped up. Without knowing anything about me, or taking time to learn about me, he greeted me with, "Praise the Lord." Before I had a chance to inform him that I, too, was a Christ-follower, he looked me square in the eye and asked, "Are you saved?" He might as well have asked me if I had sex with my wife last night. Everything in me was repulsed by his bold, unnatural, insensitive intrusion into this intimate area of my life. I left his place with a check in hand for my dad and a reminder of what it feels like to be skewered by a "spear fisherman for Jesus."

Nineteenth-century author C.N. Bovee wrote, "Kindness is a language the dumb can speak and the deaf can hear and understand." Theologian William Barclay shed more light on this subject when he said, "More people have been brought into the church by the kindness of real Christian love than by all the theological arguments in the world."

One thing I know: No one is immune to the language of love. If we remember nothing else about Mother Teresa, let's never forget her lifelong demonstration that actions speak louder than words.

BACK-DOOR EVANGELISM

a
BOOK
to read

My friend Steve Sjogren (a fellow author of *Irresistible Evangelism*) stumbled onto this truth in the late '80s and early '90s in Cincinnati. His first book, *A Conspiracy of Kindness*, introduced Christ-followers all over the world to the idea of servant evangelism. Steve often says, "Servant evangelism is taking the initiative to demonstrate God's love in practical ways by offering to do random acts of kindness in Christ's name with no strings attached." This low-risk, high-grace way of being God's seed-flinger has had a profound impact on the body of Christ all over the world. As Steve describes it, "Deeds of love allow us to sneak into the hearts of those we serve."

As the evangelism trainer for Athletes in Action, I am constantly trying to expose our staff to a holistic picture of evangelism. My mantra is "Let's bring the whole gospel to the whole person." Historically, we at AIA have been known for our emphasis on harvesting, but every farmer knows that if you want to harvest in the fall, you must sow seed in the spring. I felt Steve's model would help us balance the equation. So in the spring of 2002, I invited Steve to teach the staff about servant evangelism.

Our national headquarters had recently moved to Xenia, Ohio. The local newspaper, the Xenia Daily Gazette, had just run a front-page story to introduce us to the locals. The timing couldn't have been better for us to get out in the community and serve our way into people's hearts. As my friend Steve Bowen likes to say, "Outsiders define us by what we do, not by what we say or by what we believe." Servant evangelism is a powerful way to redefine Christianity to our communities.

I divided our group of 20 into two teams of 10. One group went to a strip mall on the edge of town. Its assignment was to wash people's windshields and refill windshield-washer reservoirs. I led the other group into the downtown business district to demonstrate God's love in the old-fashioned biblical way: by cleaning toilets. (I can think of nothing in modern times that gets closer to washing feet than that!)

> **"Outsiders define us by what we do,**
> **not by what we say or by what we believe."**

A long-time friend and fellow AIA staff member named Jim accompanied me into the Xenia Daily Gazette. We introduced ourselves to five women who were busily typing. I thanked them for the story they had run on us the previous week and explained that we were out doing something in the community that was rather audacious. We wanted to demonstrate God's love to the local business community in a practical way by offering to clean toilets.

In unison, all five ladies had a chiropractic moment: They all quit typing, jerked their heads around, and said, "What did you say?" I repeated myself as they listened in disbelief. They all agreed that no one had ever offered to serve them in this way, so they were not sure how to respond. Deciding this was a matter for the editor, they called her out and explained what we

were doing. She was touched by the offer and agreed to usher us into the newspaper's "throne rooms."

We started on the men's side first. As Jim and I were cleaning the toilets and chuckling over the whole matter, the five women barged in, and one of them shouted loudly enough for everyone in the office to hear, "They are *really doing it!*"

About that time, the editor came in and asked if another group was doing similar acts of kindness in the community. She had just received a call from someone who had encountered our other group at the strip mall. I explained what our group was doing there to demonstrate God's love to the people of Xenia.

As her editorial wheels started to turn, she asked, "Do you mind if we do a story on what you're doing?" I gave her the green light, and the next day I was pictured on the front page of our local newspaper, kneeling in front of a toilet. God's good news went out to the whole community; the article explained that we wanted the community to know that God loved them and we were just trying to demonstrate that in practical ways, with no strings attached.

I wonder what would have happened that day if we had decided to show up with a front-door approach instead. "Hi, ladies. My name is Doug, and this is my friend Jim. We decided to stop in and share the good news of the gospel with you while you work." I suspect that we wouldn't have gotten very far. Because we opted for a back-door approach, we were actually *invited* to share God's good news.

PARTNERS IN COMMUNITY

My friends Rick Rusaw and Eric Swanson, the dynamic duo from Colorado who launched the Externally Focused Church movement, describe what happened that day in this way: "Good deeds create good will, which opens the heart to the good news." These guys have taken Steve's message and de-randomized it. They challenge Christians to venture outside church buildings and come alongside different community agencies and institutions to serve with them in ongoing ways. This intentional commitment to show up day after day provides innumerable opportunities for spiritual conversations to happen naturally.

I witnessed the effectiveness of Rick and Eric's approach firsthand during another training session I was leading for our interns and our new staff

for Athletes in Action. We decided to partner with the local fire department to demonstrate God's love in a practical way to the city of Xenia. We explained to the fire chief that we wanted to bless the elderly in our community by replacing the batteries in their smoke alarms for free. He was genuinely moved by our offer. Our local Wal-Mart also loved the idea and donated the batteries.

The fire department already knew where most of the elderly resided, which is the beauty of partnering with a local institution. There's no sense in reinventing the wheel or spending time doing homework that's already been done. We provided the initiative and the manpower; they provided the maps and the fire trucks to drive us around the city. When we approached a senior citizen's door with a fireman by our side, nobody asked us who we were or why we were doing this. Our purposeful partnership gave us instant legitimacy.

Once we were in the door, our act of kindness served as the key to open a more important door: the heart. The firemen listened to our spiritual conversations and watched as we prayed for the needs we discovered through our conversations. They were now a part of something bigger than themselves; they were experiencing God Space. So guess what happened next?

While we were driving around, one of the firemen began to open up about the problems he was having in his life. What he had just witnessed had given him the confidence to do something most guys just don't do: admit weakness. This wouldn't have happened if he hadn't felt safe. The spiritual conversation that followed flowed naturally out of our shared experience. Over the next couple of weeks, our interns continued to meet with this man, and within a month, they had the privilege of leading him to Jesus.

ONE SEED AT A TIME

You may have heard it said that truth separated from experience leaves room for doubt. When we show up in our Monday-through-Saturday worlds with our Jesus glasses on and begin to notice needs and then meet them—with no strings attached, no invitations to church, and no gospel tracts—the world around us begins to experience the kingdom of God in a tangible way. The invisible becomes visible, and God Space is created.

Over time, even skeptics and cynics take note of something they intuitively know is not of this world. Seeds of curiosity are planted that grow into intrigue. This intrigue eventually gives way to an internal quest to comprehend something that is otherworldly, tapping into the eternity God has already put in each person's heart.

Brian McLaren acknowledges the power of this process in his church. In an interview, he said, "We emphasize that to be a good member of our church, we must get to know our neighbors. We say, 'Throw parties. Have people over. Be nice to the children in your neighborhood. Be good people. Be good neighbors. That makes it easier to talk to people about your faith.' You know that verse in 1 Peter 3 about always being ready to give an answer? Well, that implies that people are asking questions. To me, part of the issue is how we can help Christians live such good lives that people want to ask questions."

Don't be surprised when people begin to raise questions to satisfy their spiritual fascination. God has put this in our DNA—and in theirs, too. We truly can serve our way into spiritual conversations that happen naturally, if we don't overlook the power of kindness described in Romans 2:4: "Or do you show contempt for the riches of his kindness, tolerance and patience, not realizing that God's kindness leads you toward repentance?" Some people need to be worn down by one act of kindness at a time.

I met a "man's man" who described how his wife did just that. Year after year she wore this resilient, stubborn, strong-willed, mountain-man kind of a guy down by living out the truth of 1 Peter 3:1-2: "Wives, in the same way be submissive to your husbands so that, if any of them do not believe the word, they may be won over without words by the behavior of their wives, when they see the purity and reverence of your lives." She *prayed* it on him rather than *laid* it on him. Her good deeds were a natural way to put legs on her prayers for her husband. Over time, her consistent lifestyle—combined with God's answers to her prayers, answers that her husband couldn't refute—drove him to God. He finally gave in one night after experiencing another answer to one of his wife's prayers. The magnetic pull of the kingdom, experienced one snippet at a time, led him to repentance.

FOLLOWING THROUGH

If our good deeds create a road for our good news to travel, let's finish the trip. The church's purpose isn't to train up experts in social work. As bad as they are, poverty, injustice, world hunger, and poor health are not life's biggest issues. Where one spends eternity is! If we lose sight of this, our service will be no different from that of the Peace Corps, Boy Scouts, or Habitat

for Humanity. These are all fine organizations doing great things, but they aren't intentionally seeking to address mankind's greatest need by offering God's greatest gift to unworthy recipients (which include us).

This is why we must bring the whole gospel to the whole person. If we don't, church history will simply record one more example of what happens when the pendulum swings from an overemphasis on words, to an overemphasis on deeds, and then back again. I don't think God ever intended for good deeds and good news to be an either/or proposition.

> *If our good deeds create a road for our good news to travel, let's finish the trip... We must bring the whole gospel to the whole person.*

In the early church, gospel demonstrations and gospel declarations went hand in hand. In Acts 14:8-17, the Apostle Paul realized that his good deed had been misunderstood. He went to great lengths to make sure everyone in the crowd that day understood that *God* was the source of the good deed. Good deeds and good news were synonymous with the whole gospel Paul was sent to preach. We need to know when to bring each.

Steve Sjogren says, "Good deeds are not enough on their own to bring someone to Christ, but they do create 'phone wires' for transmitting the spoken message." When this happens we must be ready, in season and out, to share the good news. E. Stanley Jones probably described this tension between good deeds and the good news as well as anyone. He said, "The social gospel divorced from personal salvation is like a body without a soul. The message of personal salvation without a social dimension is like a soul without a body. The former is a corpse; the latter is a ghost."

Folks in the good-deeds camp love to validate their position with this quote attributed to St. Francis of Assisi: "Preach the gospel at all times and when necessary use words." My question is this: When does it become necessary to use words, in order to avoid becoming the corpse E. Stanley Jones describes?

Isaiah 28:24-26 gives us a big clue: "When a farmer plows for planting, does he plow continually? Does he keep on breaking up and harrowing the soil? When he has leveled the surface, does he not sow caraway and scatter

cummin? Does he not plant wheat in its place, barley in its plot, and spelt in its field? His God instructs him and teaches him the right way."

As I work my way through this passage, I come away with two big ideas to help answer the question. First, a good farmer is committed to the whole process from beginning to end. Second, he can be assured that while he is involved in the process, God will give him the wisdom he needs to harvest. The simple answer to my question, then, is that God will tell you when to speak if you're committed to seeing his plan through. After 25 years of being God's farmer all over the world, I've learned to discern when people are ready for words, and that is when I speak.

How do you know they're ready? Whenever their spiritual curiosity, aroused by our good deeds, causes them to move toward us. Isn't that the big idea in 1 Peter 3:15, where we are exhorted to "always be prepared to give an answer to everyone who asks you to give the reason for the hope that you have"?

Yes, we need apologetics today. But let's start by offering the incarnational proof first, and then maybe we'll have a chance to explain the hope that is within us. This is what Ravi Zacharias meant when he said, "In a postmodern culture, we need an apologetic that is felt and seen, because if postmoderns are not feeling it, they are not believing it."

Offering to pray for those we are serving is a very tangible way to provide such an apologetic. When we combine service and prayer, God Space is almost always created instantaneously. If I'm patient enough, sooner or later the recipients of God's grace begin asking me the kinds of questions that naturally allow me to explain the hope that's within me.

When we combine service and prayer,
God Space is almost always created instantaneously.

Steve Bowen is my hero in this area. One day during the Christmas season, he and I were out demonstrating God's love in practical ways to local business owners in Beavercreek, Ohio. We wanted to thank them for the contributions they were making to the local community, so we went store to store carrying tastefully decorated bags stuffed full of classy items as well as some Christmas goodies. We had no way of knowing when we walked into the Oreck Vacuum Cleaner store that day that our good deed, combined

with a word of prayer, would leave Betty (the lady working the floor that day) feeling as if she'd been in the presence of God. It was a moving experience for all three of us. Here's the replay of how God Space was created that day.

Steve and I walked into the store and greeted Betty, who was working by herself. We explained to her what we were doing and why we were doing it, and she thanked us for our kindness. Steve asked Betty if she was looking forward to Christmas. Betty hung her head, and with a sad voice told us, "Not really." I asked if there was something going on in her life that was keeping her from entering into the joy of the season.

Within seconds, Betty opened up and told us that she was considering leaving her husband after 28 years of marriage. Our hearts welled up with compassion. We asked Betty if she'd be comfortable if we prayed for her and her situation. As God had ordained it, there were no customers in the store to make her feel uncomfortable with our offer. She quickly agreed.

Steve and I placed our hands upon her shoulders and began to pour out our hearts for Betty and her situation. Betty sobbingly looked up after we were finished and asked if we were angels. She explained that she was so depressed that she had been tempted to call in sick for work that morning, and she went on to say that this was the nicest thing anyone had ever done for her.

The good will created by our good deed and prayers opened Betty's heart. She asked us what church we were from, because she wanted to bring her kids to a church where people did things like this for others. The invisible kingdom had become visible, and Betty had felt it for herself.

If you'd like to see what happens when a whole faith community brings the whole gospel to the whole person as Steve and I were able to do that day, head to Cedarcreek Church in Perrysburg, Ohio. Every four months this church baptizes 75 to 100 new Christ-followers. The last time I was there, I was touched by something they were offering to all the single moms in the area. On a Friday night after a long week of work, single moms were invited to the church for a night of pampering. Two hours of free childcare were provided, along with fancy hors d'oeuvres, manicures, pedicures, facials, and full massages while relaxing music played in the background.

I can't think of a better way to demonstrate Jesus' words in Matthew 11:28: "Come to me, all you who are weary and burdened, and I will give you rest." For two hours on a Friday night, heaven came near. The church served its way into these single moms' hearts. I can't imagine any woman leaving

that night muttering, "I'll never come to this church again." Or "I'll never again talk to people who treated me like this."

On the contrary, the Lord is adding to Cedarcreek's number those who are being saved, just as he did in the early church. Why? Because the people of Cedarcreek are bringing the whole gospel to the whole person. They're serving their way into spiritual conversations. They refuse to let their ministry be a ghost or a corpse. They are the church, and they are creating God Space in the greater Toledo area.

From INFORMATION to TRANSFORMATION

WEBSITES
to
check out

- ServantEvangelism.com
- externallyfocusednetwork.org
- stevebowen.blogspot.com
- KindnesstoGo.com
- outwardfocusedlife.com

an
APPLICATION
to make

Prayerfully peruse the ideas on the websites above. Choose one idea that you believe God would like you to act on.

a
BOOK
to read

Group's Body-Building Guide to Outreach (Group Publishing, 2006)

CHAPTER 5

Listening Your Way Into Spiritual Conversations

My date and I eased into the back pew just before the bride and the groom (my first cousin) walked down the aisle as man and wife. I sat there fuming, embarrassed, and emotionally unable to join in the day's festivities—all because I had refused to listen to my date when she suggested we pull over and ask for directions. For a full hour, I had insisted we weren't lost.

At times I'm reminded of this embarrassing incident as I lead workshops all over the world. Many seasoned believers are unwilling to admit that they may also be lost—not eternally or spiritually, but lost in their ability to connect with the not-yet-Christians in their lives. The Christians who refuse to let go of their old evangelizing maps seem convinced that they know where they're going and how to get there, despite increasing evidence to the contrary.

This doesn't necessarily mean that we have to throw away our old maps (although it could), but it *does* mean that we need to start with an attitude of humility. Times change; cultures shift. If we aren't willing to pull over to ask for directions from those we're trying to reach, we'll miss the hearts of the very people God wants us to connect with.

Have you ever moved to a new city and found yourself getting lost—*a lot*? Did it ever occur to you that while you were getting lost, you were actually becoming familiar with the city in ways that would help you find your way in the future? Didn't Jesus encourage us to be a seeking, asking, and knocking kind of people? Are you starting to see how this metaphor might help us start and continue spiritual conversations with others?

For the first 15 years of my ministry with Athletes in Action, I routinely approached spiritual conversations with this question in the back of my mind: "What do I need to say to these lost people to help them get on the right track?" I realize now that this attitude set me up to habitually commit several misdemeanors that greatly hindered the possibility of divine dialogues. In this chapter, I'd like to explain how Spirit-led listening has helped me get past these misdemeanors, and why this kind of listening is essential if we want to see the quality and quantity of our spiritual conversations increase.

HIJACKING THE CONVERSATION

The first evangelistic misdemeanor I committed regularly was hijacking the conversation, steering it in the direction that I thought would achieve my goal. If they were "lost" and I was "found," it seemed reasonable that I should do most of the talking. I realize now that these were not really spiritual conversations; they were monologues. It never occurred to me that in most of these settings, I was lost as well. I had no idea of their needs or what God might have already been up to in their lives because I was unwilling to pull over, ask for directions, and then *listen* to those directions.

Todd Hunter, the former CEO of Alpha USA, said this about listening: "I'm willing to bet the farm that in our postmodern Christian society the most important evangelistic skill is listening."

Say *what*? Most of the evangelistic training I'm aware of says very little about listening. The focus is on what we're supposed to *say*. At best, most of the Christ-followers I know practice only one type of listening: reactive listening. When we hear something we disagree with or that doesn't square with our sense of theological correctness, we react—either defensively or offensively.

Unfortunately, the Christian faith tends to be exported in the same way it was imported. Those who come to faith in the church get used to a steady diet of gospel monologues. They presume that if they approach their friends outside the church in the same way, they'll get the same results. But according to Hunter, "People used to listen their way into the kingdom. Today people are more apt to observe and talk their way into it." My experience confirms this.

We have generations of Christians—including church leaders—who

know how to give gospel presentations, but are lost when it comes to having spiritual conversations. Most of our clergy are comfortable behind the pulpit because they are in control of the conversation. However, many pastors have confessed to me how woefully inadequate they feel when they attempt to have spiritual conversations with those who don't show up on Sundays to hear their sermons.

If people aren't coming to us to have spiritual conversations on our terms, we must go to them and give up our need to control the conversation. My whole ministry changed for the better when I began to seek to understand before I sought to be understood.

EXCEEDING THE SPEED LIMIT

The second evangelistic misdemeanor I committed regularly was exceeding the speed limit—dumping all the information I knew on anyone who showed even a little interest in spiritual things. Because I was doing very little listening, I often raced ahead with more information than my listeners could handle. When we oversupply people with spiritual truth, we can kill the demand. It took me years to realize that when it comes to spiritual conversations, often more is less, and less is more.

Galatians 5:25 urges us to "keep in step with the Spirit." When we exceed the speed limit, we're getting ahead of the Spirit's work. Spirit-led listening requires us to listen to the still-small voice of the Spirit as we listen to others. The Spirit will pull us over and correct us if we aren't observing the speed limit.

> *When it comes to spiritual conversations,*
> *often more is less, and less is more.*

FAILING TO OBSERVE THE SIGNAL

The last misdemeanor happened at the "intersections" of my relationships. Sometimes I proceeded when I should have stopped, stopped when it was time to go, or recklessly moved ahead when I should have exercised caution. According to Ecclesiastes 8:6a, "There is a proper time and procedure for every matter." If we aren't listening with one ear inclined toward heaven and the other ear trained on the person in front of us, we'll run stop signs, miss divine opportunities, or even wreck a few relationships along the way. Proverbs 18:13 sums it up this way: "He who answers before listening—that is his folly and his shame."

SPIRIT-LED LISTENING

Nothing creates God Space faster than Spirit-led listening. When we demonstrate that we are truly seeking to understand people—not simply change their points of view—we create a safe environment that allows them to open up at a deeper level. As others feel genuinely understood, they also begin to better understand themselves.

Perhaps the greatest value of Spirit-led listening is that it communicates true humility and sends this powerful message: "I accept and respect you." In a self-centered, what's-in-it-for-me kind of world, Spirit-led listening will cause you to really stand out. Think about it: When was the last time *you* were listened to in a nonjudgmental, agenda-free, compassionate way?

Nothing creates God Space faster than Spirit-led listening.

a **BOOK** to read → *How Will They Hear If We Don't Listen?* by Ronald Johnson (B&H Academic, 1994)

At the same time, I'm not suggesting that we simply nod and murmur "uh-huh, uh-huh" again and again. The kind of listening I'm advocating is anything but passive. It's a sensitive but assertive quest to truly understand someone else. It requires you to probe, explore, and reflect back what you've been hearing, so that you truly understand what's been revealed to you. This kind of listening seeks to discover people's stories, to learn what interests them, to understand what turns their crank. After you've demonstrated that you're a "safe" person, most people will eventually come to share their struggles, their doubts, and even their beliefs and unbeliefs about God.

HOW WELL DO YOU LISTEN?

The quality of your listening skills powerfully affects your potential to increase the quality and the quantity of your spiritual conversations. Complete the following statements as honestly as you can.

When others are talking to me...

1. I find myself finishing their sentences.
   __ rarely   __ occasionally   __ often   __ usually

2. I give my opinions before hearing them out.
   __ rarely   __ occasionally   __ often   __ usually

3. I get restless and impatient.
   __ rarely   __ occasionally   __ often   __ usually

4. I lose track of what is being said.
   __ rarely   __ occasionally   __ often   __ usually

5. I fidget with objects.
   __ rarely   __ occasionally   __ often   __ usually

6. I mentally rehearse what I'm going to say next.
   __ rarely   __ occasionally   __ often   __ usually

7. I take control of the conversation.
   __ rarely   __ occasionally   __ often   __ usually

8. I interrupt with frequent comments or questions.
   __ rarely   __ occasionally   __ often   __ usually

9. I am suspicious of hidden agendas.
   __ rarely   __ occasionally   __ often   __ usually

10. I try to immediately diagnose their problems.
    __ rarely   __ occasionally   __ often   __ usually

11. I worry about how to respond, instead of listening.
    __ rarely   __ occasionally   __ often   __ usually

12. I tell them how to fix their problems.
    __ rarely   __ occasionally   __ often   __ usually

13. I listen briefly and then begin talking.
    __ rarely   __ occasionally   __ often   __ usually

14. I tend to contradict what has been said.
    __ rarely   __ occasionally   __ often   __ usually

15. I misinterpret what has been said.
    __ rarely   __ occasionally   __ often   __ usually

16. I answer before gaining real understanding.
    __ rarely   __ occasionally   __ often   __ usually

If you answered "often" or "usually" to three or more of these questions or if you answered "occasionally" to eight or more, you could benefit dramatically by improving your listening skills. At the end of this chapter, I'll share some extremely valuable resources to help you in this area.

Right now, though, let's look at another story that can serve as a case study for applying the principles for creating God Space.

STEPPING OUT AND ENTERING IN

When traveling to my workshops, I love to invite along people who are hungry to learn how to live outwardly focused lives in an inwardly focused world. On one occasion, I was invited to a medium-sized midwestern town. Anthony, one of our Athletes in Action staff members, went with me. We arrived a day early to speak with the leadership of the church and ensure everything was set up for the next day. Over dinner that night, the church's outreach director expressed a desire to experience some of what I was going to be talking about the next day. So I suggested we drop in on one of the local bars.

Principle 1: *Go.*

The Great Commission begins with a two-letter word: go. Listening begins with a heart that's willing to move toward the people in our lives. While I don't frequent bars as a way of life, I have learned that the best spiritual conversations usually occur in places where others feel comfortable. The church, on the other hand, communicates to the world, "If you come to us, we'll listen to you—in our buildings, on our timetable, if you use our language and dress and act as we do." The "come and see" approach of most churches is far from the "go and be" mentality modeled by the church in the book of Acts.

None of us knew what we were in for that night. Picture this: A white guy in his late 40s (that would be me), a white guy in his mid-60s (that would be the outreach pastor), and an African-American guy in his mid-30s (that would be Anthony) walk into a country bar called Stepping Out on a Friday night. A second after stepping in, I was ready to step out. I was old enough to be the father of most of the clientele, the outreach pastor could have been their grandpa, and Anthony was probably the first and last African American to set foot in this bar, as the town had very few African Americans in it. You can't imagine three guys more out of their element. Everything within me was screaming to turn around and call it a night so I could be fresh for the next day.

Principle 2: *Significant spiritual conversations usually occur when you least feel like having them.*

Any time you feel anxious, fearful, uncomfortable, or downright scared to death, there's a good chance that a significant spiritual conversation is waiting for you on the other side of those feelings—if you don't give in to them. In Luke 9:23-24, Jesus states that we must lose our lives to find them. Listening requires us to die to ourselves and our agendas. If you are waiting for this to feel natural before you do it, please give up that notion. Dominating the conversation, peppering people with too many questions, jumping to negative conclusions, and promoting your particular church often feel much more comfortable and natural than Spirit-led listening. However, the good news is that the more you die to yourself and listen as God intends, the more God will increase your capacity to care. And the more people sense that you genuinely care, the more they will welcome your invitation into God Space!

After sitting down at the bar and ordering soft drinks, we were approached by a couple of pool players who asked if we wanted to play. Anthony and I said "sure." Being Athletes in Action staff, we managed to quickly earn some credibility on the pool table with a few wins.

Principle 3: *God will use all your experiences to create God Space.*

Common ground is usually the best place to start when attempting to forge a relational connection. You'll find no better book to read on this topic than Tim Downs' Finding Common Ground.

a
◄ **BOOK**
to read

Our time at the pool table allowed us to loosen up as we chatted with our opponents. It didn't take long before they stated the obvious: "Hey, we've never seen you guys before. Are you from around here?" I told them it was our first time in their town. They asked me what we were doing there. I laughed and said, "You wouldn't believe me if I told you." Intrigued, they told me to give it a shot. I told them that one of the bigger churches downtown had invited me to speak the next day. Then I asked them if they'd be willing to help me out.

Principle 4: *Good questions create great opportunities for listening.*

I'll address this principle in more detail in the next two chapters.

Several others in the bar overheard our conversation and gathered around. I mentioned that sometimes churches are not very clued in to how

they are coming across in a community because they talk more than they listen. I said, "You could help me—and them—by telling us about your experiences with the church."

Principle 5: *Get lost in order to get found.*

Here is a perfect example of what I mentioned earlier in this chapter. I didn't know where the conversation was going, so I asked them for directions.

The bartender caught wind of our conversation and turned down the music. Pretty soon everyone had pulled up a chair around the pool table, as one by one, these people began to share stories about how they had been wounded by the church in one way or another. The bartender said she stopped going to church after she was told that her miscarriage was a result of the sin in her life. Another person said he used to teach Sunday school, but stopped because the church was always asking for more money. For 30 minutes, we listened reflectively as these people, who had been strangers an hour before, shared their true hearts with us.

Principle 6: *Validate before moving on.*

Always verify what you thought you heard by reflecting back the thoughts and feelings of the people you're listening to.

Reflective listening can be a powerful device to help you hear what people are *really* saying. Spend some time reading the Reflective Listening Phrases that follow. Make these ideas a part of your spiritual conversations.

REFLECTIVE LISTENING PHRASES

- **So, if I'm hearing you right** [briefly paraphrase the feelings and ideas you thought you heard].
- **Let me make sure I'm tracking with you. You're** [briefly paraphrase the feeling and ideas you thought you heard].
- **You're saying you feel** [briefly paraphrase the feeling] **because** [briefly paraphrase the thought]. **Is that right?**
- **Wow! You're really** [briefly paraphrase the feeling] **when you think about** [briefly paraphrase the thought].
- **What you really want me to grasp is that** [briefly paraphrase the feeling and ideas you thought you heard].

> - **It's like** [use a word picture to convey the feelings or ideas you thought you heard]. **Does that capture it?**
> - **So what ticks you off the most is** [briefly paraphrase the feelings and ideas you thought you heard].
> - **So what excites you most is** [briefly paraphrase the feelings and ideas you thought you heard].
> - **So the really big thing for you is** [briefly paraphrase the feelings and ideas you thought you heard].

The youngest person in the bar saved the best for last. First she made everyone promise not to tell anyone what she was about to divulge. Then she said that her dad, who was the owner of the bar, used to be a pastor. He had left the ministry when the church he had been pastoring split. No one at the bar had been aware that their drinking buddy, the bar owner, was at one time a man of the cloth. After everyone picked their jaws up off the floor, this young lady proceeded to shock Anthony and me by saying, "You know, I've asked a lot of people this question, but no one has been able to answer it. Could you guys tell me if it's possible to know for sure that if you died, you would go to heaven?"

Principle 7: *When God Space is created, be prepared for people to share their deepest hearts.*

Forty-five minutes had elapsed before the Spirit-led listening that Anthony and I had done paved the way for this question. For a moment, we looked like two deer caught in the headlights. I think we were initially blown away that she was asking this question in a bar on a Friday night to two guys she had just met. After recovering, we answered her question. This prompted a divine dialogue that went on for another half-hour. Questions about sin, hypocrisy, forgiveness, and salvation started to fly around.

Principle 8: *When you're invited to speak, be brief.*

Divine dialogue happens when we continue to keep the spotlight on others and what they want to talk about. Meaningful spiritual conversations happen when we accept where people are in relationship to God, even if we'd like them to be somewhere else.

We walked into that bar as strangers, but we left feeling like fellow sojourners, who had the privilege of telling spiritually thirsty people where they could find a drink that would truly satisfy them. We had, in fact, listened our way into a spiritual conversation. God Space had been created! We were invited to come back the next night for karaoke. We had become "friends of sinners."

Principle 9: *One way to tell if you've truly connected heart-to-heart is if you're welcomed back.*

Many theologians call the book of James a book on practical religion. It should be no surprise, then, that in James 1:19b all Christ-followers are urged to be quick to listen but slow to speak—just as we were in that bar.

Imagine what would happen if all Christians showed up in the culture with fewer words, and with ears eager to listen. I think we would discover what doctors today have known for a long time, thanks to a young French physician named Rene Laënnec. In 1816, Dr. Laënnec fashioned a cylinder from a sheet of paper and used it to examine a patient. He discovered that internal sounds could be isolated and amplified through a tube, making examinations less intrusive and easier to interpret. This discovery paved the way for the modern-day version of the stethoscope. Doctors use this instrument because they've learned that if they listen well, the patient's body will tell the doctor how to be an instrument of healing.

I hope you see the implications for the people in your life who need spiritual healing. If you're willing to take the initiative and listen—both to the people around you and to the Holy Spirit—I don't think you'll ever wonder again how to start a spiritual conversation.

From **INFORMATION** *to* **TRANSFORMATION**

We teach people how to listen to us by the way we listen to them. If it's clear that we're truly interested in what others think and feel, most people naturally reciprocate with equal curiosity and openness toward us. If, however, they sense we don't genuinely care about what's important to them, they'll be reluctant to open up to us. The following Faith Experiments will provide you with plenty of opportunities to experience the big ideas in this chapter.

Ask some or all of the following questions (or other questions you'd like to ask) to not-yet-Christians over a one-week period.

a
**FAITH
EXPERIMENT**
to try

- What would you like to say to Christians if you knew they would listen?
- Have you ever had a Christian attempt to convert you? If so, what thoughts or feelings did that experience stir up in you?
- Have you ever met anyone or experienced anything that made God seem real to you?
- What kinds of experiences did you have with organized religion as you were growing up?
- What would it take to motivate you to give up your Sunday mornings to attend church?
- If God called you on your cell phone and gave you the opportunity to ask him one question, what would you ask him, and why?
- What do you understand the core message of Christianity to be?
- What do you find to be the most difficult thing to buy into when you consider the claims of Christianity?
- Why do you think God seems so real to some people and so unreal to others?
- If someone wanted to talk to you about God, how would you like him or her to approach you?

Afterward, share with other Christians what you learned about how outsiders view Christianity.

Sometimes in our faith communities, we become oblivious to the kind of "scent" we're giving off. If you want to better understand how you're being perceived, the best people to help you are outsiders. Ask them to come in and give you feedback on what it was like for them to be in your church. Have your leadership team take them out for a meal afterward, so they can share their observations. Check out ChurchRater.com for more information that might help you maximize this experiment.

a
**FAITH
EXPERIMENT**
to try

My friend Dave Ping and the other folks at Equipping Ministries International help church leaders and congregations across the country develop skills for connecting deeply with friends, family, neighbors, and co-workers to naturally encourage fruitful spiritual conversations. *Listening for Heaven's Sake, Quick-to-Listen Leaders,*

a highly
recommended
RESOURCE
to help you
improve your
listening skills

and Dave's most recent small-group DVD, *Trust Building,* are excellent resources that will help you learn how to listen in such a way that's genuinely appealing and ultimately persuasive.

Check out the practical training offered by Equipping Ministries International by going to equippingministries.org or calling 1-800-364-4769.

CHAPTER 6

Wondering Your Way Into Spiritual Conversations

Someday, I'd love to open up the classified section of a major metropolitan newspaper and see the following ad in bold print:

WANTED: WONDERERS

Job Description: Explore the innermost space where the intellect, will, and emotions converge to form a worldview. To do this job well, applicant must be able to (1) create a relational environment safe enough for others to openly share what they believe, (2) reflectively listen, and (3) raise reflective questions to help others think through the implications and inconsistencies of their beliefs.
Benefits: Short-term fulfillment and long-term eternal rewards.
Job Security: Guaranteed, due to scarcity of specialists and practitioners in this field.

Would you interview for a job like that? I hope so! The Christian world is in desperate need of "wonderers" today. Quite honestly, this shortage befuddles me!

Of all the things you'll read in this book, this chapter holds the most promise if you truly want to see the quality and the quantity of your spiritual conversations increase. When you grasp how organic and natural it is to wonder your way into spiritual conversations, your conversations will never be the same.

More than anyone, Jesus knew that great questions lead to great thoughts. Many great thoughts are needed on the path from being a self-absorbed person to a God-centered Christ-follower. Questions help to peel back the layers of people's hearts and expose the things that stand between them and God.

THE POWER OF GOOD QUESTIONS

Having an array of questions at your disposal also helps give you a place to start a conversation and a way to find out what others are interested in talking about. Good questions invite people to search for answers, look in the mirror, and wrestle with the contradictions within their own belief systems. They also communicate respect by leading others into self-discovery. Questions create an arena for dialogue where Christians and non-Christians can ponder life and its mysteries together.

For all of these reasons, questions are usually more important than answers in our conversations. Let me say that again: In most of our conversations, questions are more important than answers.

a
BOOK
to read

Why? Because in most of our conversations, people aren't ready for the answers we'd like to share with them. As Randy Newman, author of *Questioning Evangelism*, says, "Instead of moving people closer to a salvation decision, an answer can push them further away." Ding, ding, ding, ding! I hope Randy's words ring a few bells for you as well.

In most of our conversations, questions

are more important than answers.

It sure took a long time for my bell to be rung. When I discovered the effectiveness of asking questions, my rocket lifted off the launchpad. As I learned to ask reflective questions, the quality and quantity of my spiritual conversations skyrocketed.

I call these "wondering questions" because they tap into a reservoir of curiosity that lies deep within each of us. If you want to unleash this organic power into your conversations, you may need to be reintroduced to a world you've lost touch with as you've grown older: the world of wonder.

THE POWER OF WONDER

I'm not sure why we leave this world behind or relegate it to children.

In it, we regularly experience emotions like awe, admiration, fascination, surprise, astonishment, amazement, and curiosity. That's a pretty attractive list, if you ask me. Who wouldn't want their days here on earth filled with these emotions? Wonder is the rocket fuel that launches us into the world of discovery.

I'd like you to stop for a moment and consider what life would be like without wonder. If you visited the former Soviet Union before the walls of communism came down, you'd have a clue. I did, and I saw for myself what a world without wonder looks like. It was gray. There was no color, no fascination, no surprise, no curiosity. For nearly 70 years, wonder was suppressed. The people were taught there was no God, and the culture reflected this belief by turning gray. When the seeds of wonder God put in our hearts aren't watered and don't have a plot of soil where they can freely grow, they shrivel up and die.

But let's be honest: This hasn't happened only in the former Soviet Union. Anyone whose world is dominated by dogmatic certainty—whose mind and heart are closed to any other reality—is living a life without wonder. It's easy to end up "wonderless" in a world that seems to prefer answers over questions and certainty over mystery. Most adults will readily admit that their imaginations haven't been stretched much for a long time.

Here's what I believe you'll find when you allow wonder to have its way with you in your relational connections:

- a climate of mutual curiosity in which we explore the mystery of life together, as fellow sojourners
- a tearing-down of the us-versus-them wall
- possibilities of mutual discovery
- elimination of the fear factor that keeps most Christ-followers from actively participating in spiritual conversations

In the land of wonder, we give up the notion that we need to have all the answers. We return to a humble mind-set in which asking, seeking, and knocking are normal. Wondering helps us move into spiritual conversations authentically by eliminating canned or awkward transitions. After the conversation is started, wondering acts like WD-40 to keep it going. At the end of the day, the reason wondering has so much potential is (drumroll, please) because *everybody* wonders.

Jesus tells us in Matthew 7:7 and Luke 11:9 that when people begin asking and seeking, they will begin to find, and when they begin knocking

on God's door, it will be opened to them. Ecclesiastes 3:11 says that God has "set eternity in the hearts" of all men and women. God has created each one of us to naturally wonder about things we can't fathom without asking, seeking, and (eventually) knocking on God's door for help. This built-in inquisitiveness is just waiting to be ignited.

At the end of the day, the reason wondering has so much potential is...because everybody wonders.

This point is powerfully made in a scene from the must-see movie I mentioned earlier called *The Big Kahuna*. Let's tune in to the dialogue between Phil and Larry as they sit on the couch and have an honest moment together.

> **Phil:** I've been thinking about God lately, too. Wondering.
> **Larry:** About God?
> **Phil:** Yeah.
> **Larry:** What about him?
> **Phil:** I don't know. Haven't you just wondered about God...ever?
> **Larry:** Well yeah, everybody wonders about God every now and then. Just some of us don't dwell on it, you know? I give it a place. I believe what I believe.
> **Phil:** Which is what?
> **Larry:** How...should I know?
> **Phil:** Things like that don't bother you, huh?
> **Larry:** What do you mean, dreams?
> **Phil:** Questions about God.
> **Larry:** Well, I figure, you know, I'm going to find out sooner or later. My wondering about it isn't going to change anything, and you know, in the meantime, why lose sleep? I get precious little as it is.
> **Phil:** But you still wonder, don't you?
> **Larry:** *(Pause)* I'm human, Phil.
> **Phil:** I know.

Larry would get an A+ in Theology 101. He rightly acknowledges that because he's human, it's only natural for him to wonder about God. Isn't this what the Bible tells us over and over?

When we use open-ended questions to tap into what others are concerned about or interested in, *our* wonder stimulates *their* wonder and paves the way for spiritual conversations to flow naturally. Effective wondering starts where people are, not where we'd like them to be. When we wonder out loud with people about what's important to them (their lives, careers, family, and so on), we create an open, safe, and nonjudgmental forum for authentic dialogue.

Our questions invite people to search for their own answers and naturally stimulate them toward spiritual seeking. I've seen the Holy Spirit use this "wonder power" to stir the imaginations of those who are far from God, help them make new discoveries about themselves, and nudge them one step closer toward the cross.

Sounds good, doesn't it? There is, however, a cost. Wondering requires us to give up the illusion that we can manipulate or argue people into the kingdom. If we try to force our agendas instead of zeroing in on topics people want to explore (and, incidentally, where the Holy Spirit is already at work in their lives), it just doesn't work. Manipulative approaches communicate disrespect and stifle the supernatural allure of the kingdom.

If everybody wonders, the next question we all have to wrestle with is "Am I safe enough to wonder with?" If not, reread Chapters 1 and 2. If the answer is yes, then let the wondering begin.

TWO WONDERING STORIES

I'd like to share two stories that illustrate what can happen when "wonder power" is unleashed in conversations with people dominated by dogmatic certainty. These are not your typical, everyday kinds of conversations. In fact, they represent the toughest kinds of conversations you might ever have. The first story involves an atheist; the second involves two Mormon missionaries who showed up on my doorstep. In both these stories, I talked with people whose minds and hearts were closed to any reality outside what they thought they already knew. Pay careful attention to how wonder picked the lock and cracked open the door to the possibility of another reality.

The first conversation was with a Ukrainian atheist in her early 30s. Galena had been assigned by the Soviet government to ensure that our Athletes in Action team's accommodations and travel were taken care of while we were in her city. As the director of our team, I interfaced with her daily. This gave us lots of time to talk and get to know each other. One day over lunch, I took the initiative to wonder into the spiritual area of her life. Here's the play-by-play of that conversation.

Me: Galena, is it true that all your life, you and your friends have been taught that there is no God?

Galena: It is as you say.

Me: I'm wondering if, in your quiet moments, you ever stop to think about how you and I got here, or how the earth, the stars, and the moon were created?

Galena: No, I accept the fact that the big bang just happened, and here we are.

Me: So, if I'm hearing you correctly, you believe we are the result of an extraordinary set of circumstances that caused something to evolve out of nothing.

Galena: It is as you say.

Me: Could I test a thought on you to make sure that I understand what you believe?

Galena: Yes, please proceed.

Me: *(I took my watch off.)* It sounds as if you believe our universe was at one time like this watch before it was assembled—just a myriad of parts randomly strewn around.

Galena: It is as you say.

Me: *(I laid my watch on the table.)* If I took my watch apart piece by piece, placed the pieces in a box, and shook them up before dumping them out on this table, I'm wondering what you think it would take to cause these pieces to reassemble again into a fully functional watch. For instance, what is the probability that a hurricane, a tornado, a fire, a hailstorm, a tsunami, or any other force of nature might bring this to pass?

Galena: It is impossible!

Me: I agree! This is why I'm wondering how you can be satisfied with your belief in the big-bang theory. We are so much more complex than this watch. If the watch requires its original creator to reassemble it, then doesn't it stand to reason there has to be someone or something greater than you and me responsible for creation?

Galena: I see what you mean. It takes more faith to believe in what I've been taught to believe in, than what you believe in.

A little bit of wonder expressed in a few questions opened the door to a heart that had been closed for more than 30 years. This opening caused Galena's intrinsic sense of wonder to wake from its slumber. For the remainder of our visit, she had her own wondering questions for my teammates and me. The idea that she lived in a world created by someone far superior to herself propelled her into an asking, seeking, and knocking mode.

Wondering into Galena's heart required a willingness to give up control of the conversation, an inquisitive nature, the patience to listen, and the desire to help her by raising the kinds of questions that prompted her own discovery. Wondering allowed me to authentically connect with Galena. It also gave me an authentic way to continue the conversation once it was started.

Furthermore, wondering helped me unveil God's creation story by turning Galena's ears into eyes. Let's move on to my second story.

Remember the story in Chapter 2 about the two Mormon missionaries who interrupted my football game? Let's pick up where I left off.

After they finished their awkward attempts to connect with me, I said, "I enjoy meeting people who have deep convictions and are passionate about their beliefs. You guys seem to fit that category because I'm guessing you've had a few doors slammed in your face today."

They laughed and acknowledged that this had been the case. I continued, "I'm wondering what makes you willing to risk this kind of rejection in my neighborhood."

Elder Bob and Elder Jim explained that they were passing out the Book of Mormon and inviting my neighbors to attend their place of worship. After they finished I said, "I'm wondering what good news you feel my neighbors and I are missing out on that the Book of Mormon will supply us with."

They did their best to explain that the Book of Mormon represents the rest of God's story and that Christians are missing out on it. After they finished, I summarized what I had heard to make sure I had the whole picture. I then said, "It sounds like you guys are going door to door in my neighborhood because you're convinced that my neighbors and I are missing the last piece of God's revelation, which would help us in this life and in the life to come."

They nodded in agreement, so I wondered some more. "I'm wondering, if my neighbors and I did take your book and read it and agree to come to your place of worship, could you assure us that this would put us in a right standing with God?"

After thinking about my wondering question for a moment, they both replied, "We hope so!"

I continued, "I'm wondering if you guys have this same assurance."

Again, they said, "We hope so!"

"Now you've really stirred up my curiosity," I said. "I'm wondering what more two guys like you, who have given two years of your life to spread your beliefs, would have to do in order to have this assurance. Would you need to spend more time each day going door to door? Would you need to spend more time reading the Book of Mormon? Please fill in the blank, because I'm trying to figure out how two guys like yourselves, who by most people's standards seem very committed to your beliefs, do not know for sure whether you'll spend eternity with God."

Elder Bob and Elder Jim paused and reflected. My wondering questions had penetrated their defenses and talking points. We were now thinking together, as fellow human beings, about their truth claims. I continued in this thoughtful moment to summarize what they'd been saying in my own words. I said, "Correct me if I'm wrong, but it sounds like you're asking my neighbors and me to get off the religious treadmills of our choice and jump on the model you're selling door to door. While I want to affirm you guys again for your passion and depth of conviction, I'm struggling to understand what I have to gain by doing this. By your own admission, if I jump on your treadmill and the ride ends, I'll still be left wondering whether I'll spend eternity with God."

Elder Jim looked at me and honestly said, "I see what you mean."

Wondering out loud had allowed me to avoid a standoff in this situation. Once again, it cracked open the door to two minds that had been set like concrete, thus paving the way for a heart-to-heart spiritual conversation about what one must do to be in a right standing with God.

As you can see, initiating wondering conversations is all about context. Listening carefully to what people are talking about is the starting point. As you do this, genuine questions will spring to mind if you let them. Look for questions that have the power to move people to think more deeply about their lives and the topics they're discussing.

The good news is that you don't have to force God into the picture. He is always there in the background, the foreground, or somewhere in between. You might have heard the old saying "All roads lead to Rome." Well, I like to say, "All good wondering questions eventually lead to God." At the end of the day he is *the* answer.

I hope you noticed something else in both of these stories: If you're listening well, wondering naturally happens; if you're wondering well, you'll have more opportunities to listen. In the next chapter, "God's Teeter-Totter," you'll learn how to balance these two powerful vehicles for creating God Space.

GOOD WONDERING QUESTIONS

- are born out of a desire to better understand someone.
- flow naturally out of your context and your conversations.
- demonstrate that you have listened thoughtfully.
- are open-ended and promote more dialogue and reflection.
- probe sensitively and reflectively into someone's belief systems.
- compel others to investigate the Christian life.

WONDERING IS *NOT*

- using questions to gain control of a conversation so you can get your point across.
- a set of memorized questions to herd people toward a decision you think they should make.
- a springboard from which to launch into a monologue.

GOOD WAYS TO START WONDERING

- That's an interesting perspective, I'm wondering how you arrived at that conclusion.
- If I could arrange for you to speak at my church about your impression of Christians, I'm wondering what you would say.
- I'm wondering what role religion has played in shaping your life.
- I'm wondering why the topic of God seems to stir up such strong emotions in you.
- I've thought long and hard about our last conversation; here's what I'm still wondering about.
- I'm wondering how my answer to that question made you feel.
- Your comments on the subject have left me wondering _____.
- I'm wondering what you think you'd have to give up or lose to become a Christian.
- I'm wondering what you think it would take for you to acknowledge the reality of God's existence.
- As we've been talking, I've heard you talk about several things that

seem to be missing in your life right now. I'm wondering if you're searching for something that's capable of filling those voids.

THOUGHTS ON USING THE PHRASE "I'M WONDERING"

Our wonder can be expressed in a multitude of ways, but there is something about beginning a question with "I'm wondering" that sets it apart. While anything can be overused, this phrase tends to soften the language that follows. It has the potential to instantly create God Space by demonstrating that we have been sincerely thinking about people or about something they said. It also protects us from dominating the conversation with our own worldview.

From **INFORMATION** to **TRANSFORMATION**

a FAITH EXPERIMENT to try ▶ Think of a topic that's been stirred up by the media, and ask people to share what they're wondering about the topic. Spend a couple of days thinking and praying about people's responses, and then formulate a couple of wondering questions based on what you heard. At an appropriate time, let these people know that you've been thinking about what they said, and ask permission to share what you're wondering.

a FAITH EXPERIMENT to try ▶ In a small-group setting, take turns role-playing common scenarios that people in your faith community encounter in their day-to-day lives. Corporately brainstorm wondering questions that could be used to spark conversation.

a FAITH EXPERIMENT to try ▶ Take time to ponder one conversation that you were in or that you overheard in the past week. Use it as a springboard to write down some wondering questions you would feel comfortable asking. Then turn to Chapter 11 and peruse the 99 wondering questions to help formulate more questions.

CHAPTER 7

God's Teeter-Totter

This chapter is going to be short and to the point. If you take everything from Chapter 5 on listening and balance it with everything from Chapter 6 on wondering out loud, you're ready to ride God's teeter-totter.

That is to say, if you spend too much time listening in your conversations, you'll leave people feeling as if they just left their therapist's office; on the flip side, too many questions leave people feeling as if they're standing before the Grand Inquisitor. A good balance of listening and wondering out loud creates God Space and helps a conversation move along naturally. If we're listening well, our wonder begins to percolate. If we're wondering well, then we'll get plenty of opportunities to listen. As we continue to balance these two, only God knows where the conversation might lead.

I want to demonstrate how this divine teeter-totter works. So jump on…

A RIDE ON THE TEETER-TOTTER

Several years ago, I was invited to speak in New Zealand. Howard (the initiator of my visit) and I traveled all over New Zealand during my two-week visit. About halfway through the trip, we had some much-needed time for a little rest and recreation. We were in the right place to do it: Queenstown. Howard and I opted for the gondola ride up the mountain to see the spectacular view overlooking the bay and the city of Queenstown. Afterward, we made several trips down the mountain's alpine slide before we sat down to relax and reflect on the upcoming workshops. Within a few minutes, my friends Jeff and Suzanne, who were traveling with us, walked in with someone we'd never met: Emma. Jeff and Suzanne had met her on their hike up the mountain. They sat down, and we started to talk.

If we're listening well, our wonder begins to percolate.
If we're wondering well, then we'll get plenty of
opportunities to listen. As we continue to balance these
two, only God knows where the conversation might lead.

To better help you understand what I mean by "God's teeter-totter," I'll give you a slow-motion replay of my conversation with Emma. From time to time, I'll interject coaching tips in *italics* that you might find helpful, starting right now.

Meeting new people the way I met Emma automatically creates an environment similar to that on airplanes (remember Chapter 1?). Familiarity seems to curb our sense of wonder rather than stimulate it. Over time, I've learned to cultivate my curiosity about others by fighting this tendency. Just because we know a little bit about people doesn't mean we really know what makes them tick. Proverbs 20:5 says, "The purposes of a man's heart are deep waters, but a man of understanding draws them out."

After exchanging the kinds of questions we've all learned to ask in social settings, I learned that Emma had quit her job in England several months before and was touring Australia and New Zealand. I found it interesting that she was doing this all alone. So I asked her if this was just an extended vacation or if there was some other purpose for her travel.

Never underestimate the power of noticing the small things. When a piece of the puzzle seems to be missing or out of place, a good wondering question can sometimes take you places you never could have imagined.

Emma explained that she had grown tired of her job in England and had decided to leave it to see if she could "find herself." I wondered if her travels had produced any "aha" moments so far.

Sadly, she said no, but suddenly she lit up. "I did have one experience that was quite interesting," she said. Emma explained that she had lost her keys to her rental vehicle. She was in the middle of nowhere with no one to help her. For hours she agonized over where she might have misplaced them. She felt alone and helpless. Just when despair started to creep in, someone happened along, and within a few minutes they had found her keys. Emma said that for the first time in her life, she thought there might be "someone up there" looking out for her.

Everything within me wanted to stop and fill in the blank for her. This looked like a divine opportunity for some kind of a gospel presentation. However, I had been there and done that before in situations like this. The Holy Spirit gave me self-control and patience to continue to keep the spotlight on Emma and her journey to find herself. She had not invited me to share my commentary on her experience. If I had given in to my impulse to do a good thing instead of a God thing, the conversation would probably have ended right then and there.

"Wow," I said, "that must have been a powerful experience." Emma nodded in agreement. I then affirmed her for having the courage to quit her job and head down "the road less traveled." I asked her what she was hoping to feel, know, or get in touch with to signal that her quest to find herself was over. She had no idea, so I asked her if she believed there really was a self out there waiting to be found. Again, she didn't know.

Sometimes the questions we ask cannot be answered on the spot because they require more time for reflection. In her book Fierce Conversations, *Susan Scott recommends that we "let silence do the heavy lifting" in our conversations. This should come as no surprise, as the Scriptures exhort us to be still and know that God is God (Psalm 46:10). Nevertheless, the temptation for those who are overly verbal is to fill those quiet moments with words. Sometimes the most Spirit-filled thing we can do is—how can I put this nicely?—shut up. Silence allows the Holy Spirit to work in the heart of the person we're talking to, while giving us the wisdom we need to continue our divine dialogue. That is exactly what happened next in my conversation with Emma.*

After chewing on my two questions for a while, Emma admitted she was confused and discouraged by her lack of progress toward her goal. She then expressed her deeper fear: She didn't want to go back to England as the same person who left.

> ### Sometimes the most Spirit-filled thing we can do is—how can I put this nicely?—shut up.

God Space had been created by caring about what Emma cared about. When people start to self-disclose and get real about what's happening in their hearts, it's usually a great sign that they feel safe in our presence.

This is a sacred trust. If we uphold it, we'll have more of these kinds of conversations.

I asked Emma's permission to share an illustration she might find helpful as she continued on her quest. She excitedly agreed. I asked if she had visited any art museums during her travels. She said she had. I asked if she had ever come across a painting that she just didn't get, no matter how long she looked at it. I jokingly told her that as an athlete, I didn't get *most* paintings I saw in art museums.

A good sense of humor helps everyone relax when you're talking about matters of the heart.

I suggested it would be nice if, somehow, the artist could be on hand to explain what he or she was trying to communicate through all those colors splotched together on the canvas. She agreed. I then stepped out into the God Space that had been created.

Over time, the Holy Spirit will give you a recurring sense of "oughtness" about when to bring up spiritual matters.

I said, "Emma, it sounds as if you might have opened your mind and heart to the possibility that there is a supreme being. If there is, and he created you, then you are much like the painting we spoke of in my illustration. If you are ever going to truly find yourself, you'll have to get to know your creator."

She looked at me like a deer caught in the headlights. Time stood still for a moment as this idea began to penetrate her seeking heart. "Thank you for planting this good seed in my head," she said. I couldn't have described what had just happened any better.

CLIMB ABOARD!

I know a mother who taught her daughter how to ride God's teeter-totter when the girl was 12. Every day when the girl came home from school, her mom asked her about the conversations she'd had that day. Together they would come up with appropriate wondering questions to ask. Her daughter would go to school the following day, ask the questions, and then listen to her friends' responses. Over time, jumping on God's teeter-totter became natural for her. She was always having spiritual conversations with her friends.

I watched the same thing happen to a college basketball player I led to

Christ one summer. Within a few weeks of becoming a Christian, he was applying the principles of this chapter with great success (probably because he had nothing to unlearn).

As your coach, all I want you to know is that you can do this with the Holy Spirit's help. The kingdom needs you to get out of the stands and into the game. You've been given the playbook and the handoff; now it's time to run with the ball.

From INFORMATION to TRANSFORMATION

Evaluate your conversations. Which end of God's teeter-totter are you more comfortable sitting on? If you want to increase the frequency and depth of your spiritual conversations, it's imperative to balance any lopsided inclinations you have.

a
FAITH
EXPERIMENT
to try

If you're a poor listener, reread Chapter 5. Note the things the Holy Spirit prompts you to do.

If you're struggling to ask good questions, reread Chapter 6. Scan the 99 wondering questions in Chapter 11. Start thinking about the conversations you've had recently. Begin to formulate questions that you could have asked.

If you want to experience a place where God Space has already been created and fellow sojourners gather weekly to jump on God's teeter-totter, you owe it to yourself and your faith community to check out Lifetree Café. Lifetree is a conversation café intentionally designed to make the big ideas of this book come alive in communities all over the country. Turn to page 128 to find out more about this cutting-edge idea that God is using to help Christ-followers cross the us-versus-them divide and build bridges to God's kingdom one spiritual conversation at a time.

Just remember, you will fall off God's teeter-totter again and again. That's all right. Get back on again and learn from your mistakes. Before you know it, you'll be planting good seeds in people's minds.

CHAPTER 8

Spiritual Appetizers

Our culture is inundated with snack offerings. We have snack—I mean gas— stations to make our trips more pleasant, snack bars that satisfy cravings at theaters, snack carts that help golfers make it through their rounds of golf, and aisle after aisle of snacks at the local grocery store. We even have a "snack newspaper" called USA Today!

In light of this, you'd think the Christian community couldn't possibly miss the fact that most people love a good snack! Unfortunately, most Christians I know admit that when someone shows the tiniest interest in their faith, they don't offer snacks in response, but a full-blown smorgasbord. Small inquiries get super-sized answers. All the not-yet-Christians wanted was a snack, but they got the full meal-deal instead.

If you embrace the idea that the best spiritual conversations start where people *are* in relationship to God, rather than where we'd like them to be, I think you'll find the concept of "gospel snacks" or "spiritual appetizers" (I will use these terms interchangeably) to be quite filling.

I stumbled onto the idea several years ago in my work with Athletes in Action. For many years, one of my roles in AIA's ministry was to walk athletes through the process of writing the stories of how they came to know Christ. While I still see value in sharing our testimonies, I've begun to realize that in most of our conversations, people aren't ready for our faith stories. They also might not address the needs of the people we're talking to. If we aren't careful, our testimonies can become spiritual monologues.

Proverbs 25:11a says, "The right word at the right time is like a custom-made piece of jewelry" *(The Message)*. My wife tells me that women enjoy jewelry parties because they give women the chance to make jewelry that matches the outfits they already own. Gospel snacks offer a similar opportunity. They allow us to share the right God story at the right time rather than taking a one-size-fits-all approach, which is often what a faith story becomes.

WHAT ARE SPIRITUAL APPETIZERS?

Spiritual appetizers are personal stories, no more than two minutes long, intended to stimulate spiritual thirst, keep the dialogue going, and demonstrate the relevance of Christ in our daily lives. They are real stories about how God has shown up in real and relevant ways since we've come to know him. We interject them into our conversations after we've taken the time to listen and understand which of them might best fit into the particular conversation we're having.

The Message's interpretation of Proverbs 18:13 puts it this way: "Answering before listening is both stupid and rude." We show disrespect when we offer something that wasn't asked for, or something that doesn't relate to the conversation we're having. Listening ensures that our snacks aren't being passed over for those reasons.

Likewise, per *The Message*, Proverbs 18:20 says that "Words satisfy the mind as much as fruit does the stomach; good talk is as gratifying as a good harvest." Spiritual appetizers stimulate the spiritual palate, and in most cases less is truly more! In my relationships I've found that if I notice what's going on in the people around me, find common ground, ask good questions, and listen, opportunities to share God stories are all around me.

a **SCRIPTURE** to memorize

But before I offer my snack, I always ask permission, I always keep it short (unless they ask me for more), and I always relate the story to the specific conversation. Most people thank me for the conversation and say they look forward to the next one.

If we're going to respond to the challenge found in 1 Peter 3:15-16 to always be prepared to share the hope within us, let's get started. Preparation usually requires a process! I have noticed that some people in the body of Christ resist the idea of preparing for spiritual conversations. They seem to prefer "winging it in the power of the Holy Spirit." There is certainly enough scriptural evidence to indicate that the Holy Spirit can do this through us, but arguably, this should be the exception, not the norm. Preparation helps

a
BOOK
to read

us to eliminate Christian jargon, refine our thoughts, and ensure that we're truly offering an appetizer rather than a sermon.

In his book *Just Walk Across the Room*, Bill Hybels, the senior pastor at Willow Creek Community Church in South Barrington, Illinois, writes:

> I've heard hundreds and hundreds of stories. Maybe even thousands. And I must admit, most of the time it's not very pretty. Not because people don't have a story to tell or because they are unwilling to tell their stories, but because the manner in which so many tell their stories is so appalling. I can't count how many times I've stood before a well-meaning Christ-follower while he or she stumbled and bumbled through some annoyingly exhausting, circuitous trip down Scriptural Memory Lane. Each time, the same thought floats around in my head: *If I were a person living far from God and had even a tinge of interest in this thing called Christianity, after hearing your story, I think I'd recommit myself to paganism.*
>
> Sounds a bit harsh, but I make no apologies. We all need our bells rung on this one. All of us who bear the name of Christ must improve our ability to communicate our faith stories.

From **INFORMATION** to **TRANSFORMATION**

So let's get started! You might find the following recipe helpful in preparing your spiritual appetizers. For the record, however, some of the best snacks I've ever eaten were created by people who deviated from the original recipe. So tweak it however you'd like; the best-tasting end product is what we're after.

I've found that gospel snacks are best prepared with others (in a small group or Sunday school class, for example). Your faith community provides accountability, a sounding board, and a jump-start to the creative process. Begin by asking each person in the group to share a specific area of life that has been touched by God in some tangible way: self-image, money, intimacy, life's direction and purpose, patience, handling anger, significance,

forgiveness, bad habits, marriage, stress. Continue this process until the group's well starts to run dry. It may take awhile, but the result will be a long list of God stories.

After the large-group experience, encourage each person to find a quiet place—a kitchen, so to speak—in which to begin preparing his or her spiritual snacks for consumption.

> I've found that many older Christians need help in recalling stories from the past. Scrapbooks, photo albums, journals, diaries, and anything else that would stir up these memories can be helpful.

To prepare your own appetizer, jot down the powerful ways God has changed you. Be mindful of the stories you already share when you talk about your faith journey. If you've been a Christian most of your life, or if you don't have many non-Christian friends, get help from your Christian friends who have had clearly defined, before-and-after conversion experiences. They'll be able to sort through the parts of your story that might best connect with not-yet-Christians.

Answering the following questions will also help you identify ingredients God would have you add to the mix when preparing your gospel snacks:

1. How would your family and friends have described your life before God showed up in it?

2. What phrase sums up your attitude toward life before you came to know God?

3. How did you attempt to meet the needs in your life apart from God?

4. What things motivated you most before you became a Christian?

5. Where did you find your sources of identity before you encountered Jesus?

6. What or who did God use to awaken you to your need for him?

7. What struggles, doubts, and fears did you have about making a commitment to Jesus?

8. When and how did you make a commitment to Jesus? (Be specific!)

9. How did you know for sure that a spiritual rebirth had taken place in your life?

10. What kinds of "aha's" do you remember experiencing when you were awakened to the reality of God?

11. What changes did God begin to bring about in your attitudes, actions, and appetites? Were they immediate, or did they take time? Explain.

12. As you look back over your journey to faith, what misconceptions did you have about God or Christians?

13. What Scripture verses or quotes has God used to leave a lasting impression on you?

14. What life lessons do you feel God has taught you along the way?

15. Is there one particular experience in your walk with God that left an immediate and lasting impression?

After you finish this process, it's time to serve your snacks! The following ideas are meant to help you serve them in the most appetizing way. Your faith community offers a safe place to start. Take turns sharing your gospel snacks. Give feedback about what connected and what didn't, the story's length, and so on. This will help people grow in confidence and competence, both of which are needed if they're going to start adding their snacks to the daily menu of their conversations. I've found that those who prepare the most also share the most, because they have the widest array of snacks to offer and are more comfortable offering them.

SERVING YOUR SPIRITUAL APPETIZERS

1. Share your stories with confidence and a warm, friendly smile.

2. Look the person you're speaking with in the eye when you're sharing. The eyes are the windows of the soul. If you're constantly looking at the floor or over people's heads, your confidence in the message you're sharing might be called into question.

3. Be genuine. Share your story in your normal, everyday tone of voice.

4. Make sure your language is understandable. Terms like *born again*, *saved*, *washed in the blood*, and *repented* are often misunderstood by those who don't know Jesus.

5. Remember this communication principle: First, there is what you *said*. Second, there is what you *meant* by what you said. Third, there is what each person *heard* you say. Finally and most important, there is each person's *interpretation* of what he or she heard. If people are consistently ending up with the wrong message, it might be time to return to the kitchen and rework your recipe.

6. This is a testimony, not a "preachimony" or an opportunity to get on your soapbox for God. Keep the focus on your life and on what God has

done in it. Be concise. If it takes more than two minutes, go back to the kitchen and trim the fat off your meal.

7. Never, never, never make negative statements about churches, denominations, or other people. The idea is to keep the spotlight on what God has done, not on the inconsistencies of his followers.

8. Be honest about your experiences; avoid glorifying your past or exaggerating details to make the Christian life seem problem-free or completely fulfilled. Keep it real, or keep it to yourself!

9. Ask God to give you wisdom concerning when to interject your story into a conversation. Also, ask God if you need to adapt any illustrations or language to relate better to the person you're speaking with.

10. At a party it's easy to figure out which snacks are good—just look for the empty platters. It's not quite that easy when it comes to gospel snacks. The only way you'll truly know if your appetizer hit the spot is to ask people to share, in their own words, what they thought they heard you say. You could ask questions like these: "I'm wondering if my attempt to communicate how God became relevant to my life made sense to you." Or "I'm wondering what you were thinking as I shared my story." Or "I'm wondering if anything I said resonated with you."

You might come away surprised when people thank you for satisfying their spiritual hunger with one of your stories. After a couple of experiences like that, I think you'll find yourself spending more time in the kitchen preparing for the next "Jesus party."

Maybe people aren't saying no to Jesus as much as we think they are.

Imagine what would happen if every Christ-follower willingly engaged in this practical process. We would have "walking Christian vending machines" regularly dispensing relevant spiritual appetizers that stimulate the spiritual palates of not-yet-Christians all over the world. Who knows? Maybe people aren't saying no to Jesus as much as we think they are. Instead, they might be saying no to the unappetizing ways we've been presenting him. Maybe the revival that God's family longs for will start in the kitchen!

CHAPTER 9

Bringing the Bible Into Your Conversations

Not long ago, I was invited to speak to a group of Christian students at the University of Virginia. Many of them were trying to figure out how to create God Space on Mr. Jefferson's campus. Little did these students know, a perfect example of what I had come to teach them was living in their midst.

If I had known more about Derick and his Spirit-led endeavors before I had spoken, I would have stood up in the chapel on campus that night and said, "There is one among you whose shoes I am not worthy to walk in. If you want to understand how to create God Space, go hang out with Derick. He has literally taken the message I've come to share with you to the street."

Derick and I had previously met at our Athletes in Action headquarters. He was part of an AIA track team, preparing for a summer missions trip overseas. After I finished speaking to his team, he introduced himself to me. He told me that my talk had truly resonated with his heart, and he invited me to look him up if I ever spoke on UVA's campus. I made a mental note of his invitation, because I could tell from our brief conversation that this guy was the real deal.

A couple of weeks before my visit to his college, I called Derick and told him when I would be on his campus. His busy schedule prohibited him from attending my talk that night, so we arranged to meet after I'd finished speaking. Derick said he wanted to take me to the place where he was creating God Space. How could I say no to an invitation like that?

At midnight in cold, drizzly weather, Derick took me downtown to where the street people of Charlottesville hang out. I quickly learned that God had

given this brilliant UVA student and gifted artist a passion for the "least of these" whom Jesus spoke of in Matthew 25:40-45. God Space had been created on the street because one of the cream of the UVA crop chose to regularly leave the hallowed grounds of this historic institution and hang out with those at the bottom of the social barrel. Does this sound like anybody you know?

Derick had been selected by his peers to "live on The Lawn" his senior year. There is no higher honor for a UVA student. A tradition conceived by Thomas Jefferson himself, select students are chosen to live and learn side by side with professors in the academic village called "The Lawn." Only 47 students are awarded this privilege each year.

Derick was on the track team and was involved in a host of other activities on campus that kept him busy. Nevertheless, he chose to invest his life rather than spend it. God led Derick to be a wise steward of his time, talents, and privileged position at UVA. Derick wanted the city of Charlottesville to stop turning a blind eye to these street people created in God's image. Therefore he decided to tell their stories by painting huge, larger-than-life paintings of the people who had touched his life out on the street. He was hoping that God would use his paintings to restore some dignity and respect to the "invisible people" of Charlottesville.

As we walked around, it became evident that everyone on the street knew Derick. He had become one of them, a part of their community. He regularly hung out with them, listened to them, learned from them, and helped them in any way he could. They were honored to have Derick tell their story through his paintings.

After an hour on the street, we bumped into a guy Derick had met previously. His name was Chris. The three of us did what street people do: We found one of those free newspapers, sat down on it, and talked about life on the street. The awning from a movie theatre provided shelter from the drizzle, but did little to keep us warm. After about 30 minutes on God's teeter-totter, we learned that Chris had lost his job, so he had decided to go on the road, play his guitar in little bars, and write music and poetry in a journal.

We noticed he had a Bible sitting beside his guitar case. We asked if he read it much. He explained that it wasn't his; he had picked it up for a friend who had left it out on the street the night before. He'd decided to read it just for the heck of it until he bumped into his friend again and could give it back to him. He told us that he found it a very deep but confusing book. He

had drawn this conclusion after spending a good part of the day reading the whole book of Hebrews.

When we told him we were into the Bible in a big way, he started to ask questions. It was like the story of Philip and the Ethiopian eunuch (see Acts 8:26-35). We didn't have to find a way to bring the Bible into our conversation; it was already front and center. Chris was asking the questions, and Derick and I were humbly trying to answer them in a way that a first-time reader of the Bible could understand. Derick and I were just spiritual beggars trying to share with another spiritual beggar where we found our bread. Later, after an hour-long, divinely inspired dialogue, Derick invited Chris to come in off the street and sleep in his room on the UVA campus.

We didn't get to bed until 3:30 that morning. I had a Jesus buzz that carried me through my next day of speaking engagements despite just three hours of sleep. (Be warned, God Space will do things like this to you.) I only wish I could bottle up that experience so I could share it with every Christ-follower I meet.

Derick lived out of his Spirit-filled heart. God Space started inside of him, and as the natural gave way to the supernatural, the downtown streets of Charlottesville experienced the overflow.

You and I know that Philip-and-the-Ethiopian-eunuch experiences don't happen every day. In fact, I've had only this one in 25 years of ministry all over the world. So if you're waiting for the Bible to be brought into your conversation as it was in this story, you could be waiting a lifetime. In the meantime, it seems we would all be better off if we learned how to bring the Bible into our daily conversations. But how, in a world as diverse as ours, is it possible to do this naturally?

OPEN THE BIBLE THAT'S YOU

For starters, I truly believe that if you are serving, listening, and wondering, the Bible has already been brought into your conversation, incarnationally speaking. Nevertheless, there is no substitute for God's Word. When we get people into the Bible, something supernatural happens. One penetrating Scripture that connects with a heart can be worth more than a lifetime of sermons.

Hebrews 4:12 describes what happens when we unleash this holy hurricane into our conversations: "For the word of God is living and active. Sharper than any double-edged sword, it penetrates even to dividing soul and spirit, joints and marrow; it judges the thoughts and attitudes of the heart."

a
SCRIPTURE
to
memorize

I truly believe that if you are serving, listening, and wondering, the Bible has already been brought into your conversation, incarnationally speaking.

To illustrate how natural it can be to introduce the Bible into your everyday conversations, allow me to share another story—one which bundles all the big ideas of this book together. Again, everything you'll see in *italics* represents coaching comments to help you key in on essential principles.

I had challenged some of our AIA staff to think of the hardest place they could go to do the work of evangelism. We didn't have to think for very long. Antioch College is just 15 minutes from our AIA headquarters. This school is considered one step beyond Berkeley for its disdain of evangelical Christians. Every kind of lifestyle and worldview—except Christianity—is championed there.

We were well aware that many of the students at Antioch were resistant, or downright opposed, to the gospel. If there was ever a time for a backdoor approach onto a campus where the front door was heavily guarded, this was it. In the spirit of Colossians 4:5, we decided if we were going to be wise, it would be best to demonstrate God's love to these people in a practical way. It was a hot day, so we showed up on campus with cold drinks. I approached a group of about eight students sitting outside the school cafeteria and asked them if they wanted a cold one.

One guy got really excited as he thought I might be handing out free beers. After everybody calmed down and ordered the tamer drinks I was serving, one girl looked at me and asked, "Why are you doing this?" I explained that when I was in college, somebody had demonstrated God's love to me in a practical way and it changed my life. I told her that the free drinks were just a tangible reminder of God's love, no strings attached.

She fired another question: "Whose God?"

I replied, "The God who changed my life."

She loaded her gun again. "What religion are you?"

I responded, "I hate religion. Religion is a bunch of man-made rituals and traditions designed to change you from the outside in. I'm talking about true spirituality, where God takes up residence inside of you and changes you from the inside out."

"That's cool," she said.

Grace is such a foreign concept in our world. When we come as servants

to be the gospel to others, we should anticipate and prepare for the kinds of questions people might raise. How we handle these initial questions will, many times, determine whether we have a meaningful spiritual conversation.

I immediately hopped up on God's teeter-totter and began to ask questions. I wondered what had compelled them to choose this school, out in the middle of nowhere, to pursue their college education. Each of them had fascinating stories to share, but the bottom line was, Antioch College offered them a safe place to be in community with other people who valued being open-minded.

I wondered if the school had met their expectations for open-mindedness. Interestingly enough, all of them were disappointed. They said that the school was open-minded to a point, but very close-minded toward middle-class folks living in the suburbs.

I asked them if they felt it was ever OK to just close their minds to something. This got them thinking about the bigger implications of what they were really saying.

These were things I was authentically wondering about. People have "sincerity radars," so the best wondering questions are sincere expressions of your inquisitiveness. Their answers to my questions gave me an opportunity to wonder some more, after I did some Spirit-led listening. As this conversation was going on, I was praying without ceasing, asking God for wisdom and direction.

As an example, I brought up the subject of love. I asked if they thought it was OK to close their minds to things like racism, genocide, and other forms of hatred, which are polar opposites of love. This wondering question sensitively pushed them toward the edge of seeing their worldview for what it was. I could tell they were beginning to grasp the inconsistencies of their most cherished value. While they were teetering, I decided it was time to push them over the edge.

One of the greatest ways we can serve people in a spiritual conversation is to raise the kinds of questions that help them see the inconsistencies of their worldviews. For most people, the process of repentance is not one big decision, but a series of mini-decisions. Good questions create a dissonance that compels a change in thinking.

In the spirit of Dr. Phil, I asked how the value of open-mindedness was working out for them in their relationships. I shared the following example to illustrate what I was getting at. "If you were in a committed love relationship and your partner turned to you one day and said, 'I'd like you to stay

open-minded about something. You know I love you, but I also have two other girls and one other guy I love as well. I just want to make sure you're open-minded enough to share me with these three other people.' How would that make you feel?"

For most people, the process of repentance is not one big decision, but a series of mini-decisions. Good questions create a dissonance that compels a change in thinking.

This example was appropriate in this context. A lesbian, a transvestite, and some folks who swung both ways were in this group of students. Jesus used parables that keyed into people's everyday lives. We need to do the same if we are going to engage minds and hearts in our conversations.

This question nearly threw everybody into cardiac arrest. One by one, they began to share stories about their broken relationships. My wondering questions had penetrated a main artery. I asked them to define the kind of love they hoped to find in a long-term, meaningful relationship.

When people come face to face with their belief systems and become uncomfortable with their irrationality, we need to help them imagine a preferred scenario. Our questions can help lead them toward greener pastures where the Good Shepherd is waiting to greet them with open arms.

I was shocked to hear them grapple for a coherent definition of a word they all desperately longed to experience. It sounded as if they were saying that *love* is a feeling you are going to feel when you have a feeling you haven't felt before. Sound confusing? I thought so! I asked them if I could toss out a definition for them to consider. They told me to go for it.

Patience and self-control are vital to ensure we don't impose our conclusions on the questions we raise. It takes some people a long time to perceive the inadequacies of their worldviews. When they draw a blank, sometimes we need to supply some food for thought to continue the conversation.

I defined love for them this way: "*Love* is a commitment you make to act in someone else's best interest. True love can only be known by the actions that it prompts." They all looked at me as if I were Jesus delivering the beatitudes to the masses. They were stunned by how much sense this definition made.

When our conversations scratch where people are itching, many times their hearts are opened to hear more from us.

It was time for me to bring the Bible into the conversation. The last thing I

wanted to do was leave them with the impression that I had figured this out all by myself. I said, "That's my definition of *love*, but I know of one that's far better than that. Would you like to read it for yourselves? It comes from the Bible."

When our conversations scratch where people are itching, many times their hearts are opened to hear more from us.

Always ask for permission to bring the Bible into your conversations. The Bible conjures up all kinds of wild images in the minds of non-Christians. It's extremely naive to assume that everyone has positive vibes toward the Bible.

I pulled out my PalmPilot and dialed up 1 Corinthians 13:4-7: "Love is patient, love is kind. It does not envy, it does not boast, it is not proud. It is not rude, it is not self-seeking, it is not easily angered, it keeps no record of wrongs. Love does not delight in evil but rejoices with the truth. It always protects, always trusts, always hopes, always perseveres."

After each one of them read it, one of the guys said, "That's the best definition I've ever read." One of the young ladies exclaimed, "That's cool!" The rest of the group chimed in with positive responses as well.

I believe that folks who are de-churched or seemingly apathetic toward Christianity are sending the church a clear message. They want us to demonstrate how a book written several thousand years ago could possibly have something to say to them in this day and age. I think we owe them that much, don't you? According to Willow Creek's study Reveal, *"Having spiritual conversations with seekers is the most effective strategy for personal evangelism" in the church's ministry. I think that real people talking about real faith in a relevant way is what makes sense in the real world.*

I asked the group if I could share why our conversation meant so much to me personally. They gave me the green light.

I explained that when I was in college, I had struggled to find love in all the wrong places. I went through a painful breakup with a girl I thought I would marry. The breakup caused me to take a look at my own definition of love, and I realized it sounded something like this: "I love me, and I want you to make me as happy as I can be. If you can continue to make me as happy as I can be, then I will continue in this relationship."

After reading the Bible's definition of love, I had an epiphany: If God created us, and God is the author of love, who would know better how to sustain a love relationship? This revelation caused me to see how relevant

God was to every area of my life. I began to seek him with my whole heart, and my life has never been the same.

Sometimes our spiritual appetizers need to be served up after we've introduced the Bible into our conversations, to demonstrate its reality in our own lives. Other times, spiritual appetizers create the hunger necessary to introduce the Bible into our conversations. The Holy Spirit will give us the wisdom to know which way to go on this matter.

My story spoke to the cries of their own hearts, but there was one problem. I was describing the Christian life in a way that didn't fit their perceptions of Christianity. One by one, these students shared stories of ways they had been turned off by Christians. The Bible was not held in high regard because, as far as they were concerned, it was responsible for the behavior they detested in the Christians they had met.

One of the ways you can tell God Space has been created is when not-yet-Christians feel free enough to tell you how they really feel about the faith. Never try to deny or get defensive about what they share. Just seek to understand—and if necessary apologize for—the actions of Christ-followers who have contributed to their pain.

As I respectfully listened, the young lady who had peppered me with questions earlier leaned over and said, "I like you! I like what you're doing and how you're doing it. We get most Christians thrown off this campus in 15 minutes. This is the best conversation I've had at this school since I've been here." It was not exactly a conversion, but it was a nudge in the right direction.

These open-minded free thinkers had a distorted, dark picture of Christianity before our conversation. I think God empowered me to reframe their picture of Christianity and throw some fresh color on the canvas. On this day, with this group, the Bible's stock went up, simply because I introduced the Scriptures into our conversation at the right time, on a topic they cared deeply about, and then stood back and let God's Word speak for itself.

ONE AHA AT A TIME

Brian McLaren provides a much broader scope by which to evaluate this story. He says:

> Much of our evangelism here in the United States was developed in a context of Christendom, in which just about everybody knew the basic information of Christianity and was favorably disposed to it. Evangelism

got people to act on what they already knew and, in a sense, already pas-
sively believed. You could call people to commitment relatively quickly.
You could also use pretty forceful persuasive techniques. In dealing with
postmoderns, you're dealing with people who do not know the basics of
Christianity. If anything, they have a negative idea of what Christianity is.
So it makes no sense to them if you come on too strong and quickly ask
for a commitment. We should count conversations rather than conversions, not because I don't believe in conversions, but because I don't
think we'll get many conversions if we keep emphasizing them.

In other words, spiritual conversations are more than distributions of
information dominated by our worldview. They are relational interactions,
which lead to transformation one aha at a time. In my own workshops, I
typically ask for a show of hands to see how many Christ-followers came to
faith by making one big decision at an evangelistic outreach—usually only 10
to 15 percent respond in the affirmative. In a study done by Vision New England in 2007, 86 percent of respondents described their faith as a process.
Our relational interactions inform the process that leads to transformation.
There is strong evidence here that God wants to use ordinary Christians to
advance his kingdom, one conversation at a time, one aha at a time.

You might not feel ready to pull off a conversation in a hostile setting
like the one I just described. But if you're faithful in creating God Space in
the conversations you're having, you'll have plenty of natural opportunities
to bring the Bible into those conversations. It's not as difficult as you might
think. God is the author of life; therefore, every conversation has spiritual
overtones with biblical roots. The key is introducing the Bible at the right
time, with specific references that directly apply to the conversation you are having. Proverbs 15:23 says, "A man finds joy in giving
an apt reply—and how good is a timely word!"

◄ a **SCRIPTURE** to memorize

The spirit in which you do introduce Scripture is critical. If
people sense you're trying to use the Bible as an authoritative "crowbar"
to beat them into submitting to your viewpoint, your conversation is likely
over. However, if you humbly ask for permission to introduce the Scriptures
into your dialogue, "deep spiritual magic" begins to happen. Now the Bible
becomes the fulcrum of God's teeter-totter. Your role is to help unveil the
relevance of God's Word, question by question.

Be careful not to ruin the tour with uninvited answers or an oversupply

of information. The following progression might help you imagine how it might sound to naturally bring the Bible into one of your conversations.

Ask for permission. "Would you mind if we take a look at what the Bible has to say about this? I've found that it often prompts me to see things I had never thought of before."

Have them read the passage. "Would you feel comfortable reading these verses out loud?" *There is power in the spoken word, but don't press the issue, as some people are self-conscious about reading out loud.*

Keep the focus on the passage. "After reading these verses, I'm wondering if you were surprised or intrigued by anything. Did you glean any insights from these verses that you think might be pertinent to our conversation?"

Some practical suggestions. If you aren't good at finding passages quickly, it might be helpful to carry a small topical Bible with specific Scriptures listed under each topic. Better yet, invest in Bible software that will enable you to do a quick search on your PalmPilot, Blackberry, or iPhone. Many not-yet-Christians may feel awkward if you pull out a Bible in a social setting. If you do, make sure it's a pocket-sized Bible.

GOD'S FEDEX TEAM

God is looking for a few good men and women to move quickly to distribute appropriate resources when a need has been identified in a conversation. People on this team must never forget that spiritual openness can pass quickly. Getting the right resource into people's hands at the right time can create just enough curiosity for them to start reading the Bible on their own. If you're verbally challenged and find that your processing speed is just a little slow for the kinds of conversations I've been talking about, you may be a prime candidate for God's FedEx team. The resources can do the talking for you.

Browse the shelves of a Christian bookstore or talk to Christian workers on the frontlines. After you've explained the context of your conversation, they may be able to point you to helpful resources. Just remember one of the big ideas from the last chapter: In most cases less is more. After you've secured the appropriate resource, here's how your FedEx delivery might look: "During our last conversation, you raised several matters that I felt unqualified to address. So I found this resource that you might find helpful.

I'm wondering if you would be willing to read and discuss it with me over a cup of coffee sometime?"

FROM THE BIBLE TO THE GOSPEL

Many people, including Christians, have been turned off by gospel presentations. An overzealous new believer with the four spiritual laws in hand, or a fanatical Christian using confrontational techniques, can do a lot of long-term damage. These Christ-followers always seem to have their combines running in high gear because they see every wheat field as ripe for harvest. If their passion—which is admirable—is not harnessed and balanced by God's wisdom, they eventually settle into becoming slick salesmen for Jesus. If you've ever experienced someone like this, it's easy to dismiss gospel presentations by association. In spite of this unfortunate reality, I think gospel presentations are extremely relevant when people are ready to experience the new life that Jesus offers.

A good, clear gospel presentation helps seekers understand and respond to the gospel message. It's concise and to the point. Illustrations, questions, and diagrams further enhance comprehension. Different people need different tools on their spiritual journeys. Gospel presentations are just that: tools. A tool in the hand of someone who has been trained to use it can be productive.

However, let's never forget that God didn't give us a gospel presentation in the Scriptures; he gave us his Son. Jesus' approach was as varied as the people he encountered. This approach is what Jesus modeled throughout the gospels from beginning to end. So beware of well-intentioned—but misguided—believers who are convinced that one tool fits all. Jesus didn't sign off on that idea, and neither should we.

How do you know when someone is ready to move from a spiritual conversation (in which the Bible has been introduced) to a gospel presentation? My father actually helped me answer this question. In John 4:35, Jesus challenges his disciples to look at the fields because they were ripe for harvest. One day I asked my father, who is a farmer, how he knows when a wheat field is ripe for harvest. He explained that as wheat matures and ripens, the weight of the wheat grains reach a tipping point, which causes the wheat stalk to bend over. Ergo, when you look out over a wheat field and see a majority of the heads on the wheat bowed, it's harvest time.

This agricultural principle that Christ alluded to coincides with my own experience of introducing people to Christ. Second Corinthians 7:10a says, "Godly sorrow brings repentance that leads to salvation." When the head and the heart are bowed toward God in humility that comes from brokenness, it's time for the gospel. If you throw people God's gospel rope before they've come to the end of their own rope, they might be annoyed or might even disdain it. On the other hand, they'll thank you profusely when they've come to the point of realizing that they *need* God's lifeline.

You know that the wheat is beginning to ripen and harvest time is drawing near when

- seekers start initiating spiritual conversations on their own.
- the frequency and depth of their questions start to increase.
- they begin to read the Bible on their own.
- they express sorrow, dissatisfaction, or fear about the direction their lives are taking.
- they want to spend more time with you.
- they raise objections that make belief difficult for them.

This last one confuses many Christians, but don't let it. Anytime we make big, life-changing decisions, we encounter hurdles that make belief difficult, if not impossible, until we are able to get over them. This does not mean the desire isn't there. Quite the contrary; what most seekers are really trying to tell us is "I'd love to believe what you believe. If you could just help me resolve this one issue, I'm there." When we encounter people who get stuck here, it's time to take on the role of spiritual midwife. We do this by helping in any way we can to address the obstacle to faith so that the birthing process can continue.

God has called us all to be good-news people in a world dominated by bad news. Everybody we meet is a candidate for good news because everyone is either moving toward the heart of Jesus or away from it. When we bring the Bible into our conversations, we become God's mustard-seed planters. While these seeds may start out small and insignificant, when they sprout and take root, no one can predict the rest of the story.

God has called us all to be good-news people in a world dominated by bad news. Everybody we meet is a candidate for good news because everyone is either moving toward the heart of Jesus or away from it.

That's it! The next time I'm asked what I do for a living, I'm going to say I'm the chief botanical director for Athletes in Action and I specialize in planting mustard seeds. What a job title!

From **INFORMATION** to **TRANSFORMATION**

Go to AllAboutGod.com, and familiarize yourself with a resource that helps believers address the tough questions not-yet-Christians often pose in spiritual conversations.

a WEBSITE to check out

Invite a Christian friend to help you practice bringing the Bible into your conversations in natural ways. To make this as practical as possible, role-play some of the conversations you've had recently. The more comfortable you are, the more natural it will be. To help you find passages quickly, you might want to invest in a pocket-sized topical Bible, such as Thomas Nelson's *Quick Reference Topical Bible Index,* or even an electronic-format version such as the one offered for *Nave's Topical Bible Index* (Nelson Electronic).

a way to PRACTICE

Using role-playing techniques, have people in your faith community (preferably a small group) discuss specific Bible passages that describe what a person must do to become a Christian. Emphasize the idea of being a tour guide rather than a teacher or preacher. For starters, check out John 3:16; Ephesians 2:8-9; Colossians 1:21-22; Titus 3:4-7; 1 John 5:11-13; Romans 10:9-10; and John 1:12.

a way to PRACTICE

Go to your local Christian bookstore, and skim the different gospel presentations. Find a couple of resources you would feel good about sharing with someone who is ready for such a tool. Two of my favorites are *The 3:16 Promise* by Max Lucado and *Ultimate Questions* by John Blanchard.

two BOOKS to read

Find a small group of people in your faith community who are serious about having spiritual conversations. Go to your favorite coffee shop and pull out the local newspaper. Identify major stories people are talking about, and discuss how you might bring the Bible into those conversations.

a way to PRACTICE

GOD

CHAPTER 10

Reclaiming Missed Opportunities and Rebuilding Burned Bridges

This chapter is dedicated to the subject of failure. Sounds fun, doesn't it? The truth is, you will fail again and again as you endeavor to apply the big ideas in this book. Howard Hendricks, the well-known professor from Dallas Theological Seminary, used to say, "You show me a man with a bag full of successes, and I'll show you a man with a bag full of failures." Despite Paul's exhortation to Timothy to be ready in season and out of season (2 Timothy 4:2), most of the time we're not. The sooner you come to grips with this reality, the sooner you can move on to reclaim your missed opportunities and rebuild your burned bridges.

a **PRAYER** to offer →

"Lord, as I read this chapter, bring to my mind the missed opportunities that I need to reclaim and the burned bridges that I need to repair."

It took me one day to learn this lesson—but it came 22 years after I'd begun my Christian journey. I'll share the experience God used to free me from the guilt and shame that often accompany missed opportunities. The commentary in italics is intended to help you see how easy it often is to reclaim those missed opportunities.

MY RECLAMATION STORY

I started the new millennium by deciding to be my own general contractor for the construction of our new home. No other decision in more than 22 years of full-time evangelistic ministry has put me in closer day-to-day contact with rough-talking, hard-working guys who don't know Jesus. I worked, sweated, got dirty, and problem-solved with my framing crew. One day, I overhead one of the workers instructing a new guy on the job to refrain from cussing or telling X-rated "Howard Stern–type" stories around me because I was a "religious guy." These guys who were erecting the walls of my house had also begun to erect mental walls around *themselves* that would make it difficult to connect with their real hearts in a redemptive way.

Later on, as we were working, one of the guys mentioned the "C word"—church. All of a sudden, everyone began to engage in the sport of church bashing. Years ago, I might have launched into a sermon defending the virtues of going to church, but instead I said, "I'm just wondering…what kinds of experiences have you guys had that made you see church the way you do now?" Wow! My little question exploded a dam that had been holding back a torrent of emotion. One by one, they began passionately sharing stories of abuse and selfishness they had experienced from church and church people. I listened quietly, sadly identifying with much of what they said.

After our conversation about the church, the guys from my framing crew began to wonder if I was a pastor. So they asked me what I did for a living. I shared my God story to give them some context for why I do what I do. Don (the biggest guy in the crew) asked me a follow-up question after I had finished. The other guys began to poke fun at Don and asked him if he "wanted to get saved, too." Don shot them a look I will never forget and said, "What are you guys laughing at? You know you'll all be in hell with me someday."

I was tongue-tied. I'd traveled the globe preaching about how to find forgiveness and get into heaven, but I knew Don and the others well enough to recognize that an evangelistic sermon from me would end the conversation then and there. To be honest, at that moment I didn't know what to say to keep this conversation going. So I said nothing! I walked away that day feeling like I had just missed the winning field goal in the big game. What I

didn't realize at the time is that God was using my failure to teach me something that has since liberated Christ-followers all over the world. He showed me how to wonder back into a missed opportunity and reclaim it.

When we're not sure what to say or do in the moment, "nothing" always seems like the best option. Most missed opportunities fall into this category. Although it felt like failure at the time, I've since come to the conclusion that this may be the best *thing that could happen in these situations. To blurt out something, just because you don't want to miss an opportunity, burns bridges. Proverbs 12:18 says, "Reckless words pierce like a sword, but the tongue of the wise brings healing." It may be wiser to walk away from a conversation if the Holy Spirit has not given you something specific to say. This gives you time to prayerfully consider what to say later on. Here's how it played out in my story.*

Over lunch on the job site a month later, I said, "Don, I've been thinking a lot about something you said awhile back."

Intrigued, Don replied, "What's that?"

When we're not sure what to say or do in the moment, "nothing" always seems like the best option. I've since come to the conclusion that this may be the best thing that could happen in these situations.

"Well," I said, "I meet a lot of people in my line of work who are sure they're going to heaven. I don't meet many who are as confident as you are that they're going to hell. I'm wondering what makes you so sure you'll end up in hell."

I listened as Don told me the "unforgivable" things he'd done in his younger years when he was a member of a motorcycle gang. After hearing his long list of deeds that deserved hell, I said, "You sound like a condemned man with no hope of mercy or pardon. I wonder if you'd be interested in hearing what God has done to make it possible for you to be released from your death sentence."

After giving me his permission, Don listened carefully as I talked about what Jesus did on the cross to make it possible for his pardon to be realized.

Don didn't pray to receive Christ at that moment, but he concluded our conversation by saying, "Maybe there *is* hope for me." As he walked off the job site that day, our spiritual conversation had produced a nudge in the right direction.

If I had not sought to reclaim the opportunity, this conversation would never have happened. More than likely, the conversations that followed later on might not have happened either. Keep that in mind as you read the rest of the story.

Several weeks later, Don pulled me aside to tell me he'd gone with his live-in girlfriend of six years to see the movie *The Passion of the Christ* (I had encouraged him to go). When I asked him what he thought of the movie, he replied, "It really messed up my life. My girlfriend just gave her life to Christ, and now she wants to get married and go to church every Sunday!"

I reflected, "So it sounds like you're upset because your girlfriend has changed so much that you're not sure who you're really living with anymore. I'm wondering what's holding you back from doing what she did so you can both enjoy this new life together."

Don immediately confessed his inability to clean up his own life, adding that he didn't want to become like the people in the church he disdained, the "hypocrites."

I replied, "Don, I'm wondering if you believe God is big enough to do what you know you can't do on your own."

"I've never thought of it that way before," Don said.

Once again our spiritual conversation had prompted a change in the way Don was thinking about himself and in the way he was thinking about God.

As my home neared completion, Don and the crew came back to finish up some odds and ends. When no one else was around, he told me he had gone to church at Easter. This was quite a paradigm shift from the Don I had started the job with three years earlier. He actually admitted to enjoying the service.

If your curiosity has been aroused, I should tell you that Don hasn't made a decision to follow Christ yet. He has, on his own initiative, come to hear me speak on two occasions. Just recently, eight years after our first spiritual conversation, Don promised me he would read Max Lucado's *The*

3:16 Promise. (This 64-page booklet clearly explains the gospel; I recommend it highly.) I can't tell you the rest of the story unless Don comes to Jesus before this book goes to print. But aren't you wondering how much longer it will take for the eternity God put in Don's heart to catch up with him? I am!

an
APPLICATION
to make

As you read this story, did God bring a missed opportunity to mind? If so, maybe it's time to put the book down and apply what you just read. Who knows where the Spirit's reclamation work might lead you?

The good news is that most of our failures can be reclaimed. There's no statute of limitations. In most cases though, the sooner the better.

The bad news is that there are some missed opportunities that can never be reclaimed. Deathbed scenarios and one-time meetings fall into this category. That is why we must rely on God's grace and learn from our failures, strengthening our resolve to never let this happen again.

The good news is that most of our failures can be reclaimed. There's no statute of limitations.

a
SCRIPTURE
to
memorize

"So be careful how you live. Don't live like fools, but like those who are wise. Make the most of every opportunity in these evil days" (Ephesians 5:15-16, NLT).

REBUILDING BRIDGES OTHERS HAVE BURNED

Recently I had a chance to rebuild a bridge that somebody else had burned. One day, my painter was finishing some work in my house. I was in the same room, preparing for an upcoming workshop. He asked me what I did for a living, and I explained that I was an author and speaker.

I asked him if he would be willing to help me do what I do better. After he agreed, I asked if any Christian had ever attempted to evangelize him. Without hesitating, he told me about a guy he had worked with for a long time who, one day, came to work and hit the "nice switch." This caused my painter to wonder what was up. Then the guy went into his church-salesman routine, extolling the virtues of his church.

I asked my painter how the experience had left him feeling. He said it felt really creepy. He began to realize that this guy had an agenda in their relationship. He never took the time to ask my painter any questions about his church or spiritual background. He just launched into his presentation without ever listening. My painter later found out that his co-worker's church was having a hard time financially, so it had embarked on a membership drive to alleviate the problem. He felt as if he'd been targeted. He concluded by saying that the whole experience had turned him off church and religion.

I'm telling you this story because America is full of de-churched people and people like my painter who never want to be churched because of these kinds of experiences. Not only do we need to rebuild the bridges we've burned, we also need to rebuild the ones others have burned, one humble apology at a time.

That's what I did that day with my painter. As a member of the Christian community, I reached across the divide and assured him that his experience did not reflect the heart of Jesus. I apologized and encouraged him not to hold Jesus responsible for something one of his followers had gotten wrong. (The DVD *Lord, Save Us From Your Followers* documents what happens when we practice "apologetics" this way. It can be found at lordsaveusthemovie.com.)

a **MOVIE** to watch

As a result, my painter's heart opened, and we had a great spiritual conversation. Some of the damage had been repaired. He left our conversation with a new understanding of the difference between religion (which he disdained) and true spirituality (which he was now curious about). I left our conversation with another reminder of what can happen when you and I are willing to rebuild burned bridges.

From INFORMATION to TRANSFORMATION

Now that you have a reclamation plan, let's focus on how to do the work of rebuilding. Anytime we kill the potential for spiritual conversations in the ways I described in Chapter 2, we run the risk of burning a bridge. Unfortunately, if we do not do something to rebuild the bridge, it could very well remain broken for a lifetime. It's unrealistic to think that the bridge

a
SCRIPTURE ▶
to meditate
on
is going to be rebuilt from the other side. *We* need to make the first move, with an attitude similar to that of the Apostle Paul's: "I strive always to keep my conscience clear before God and man" (Acts 24:16).

If, as you read Chapter 2, you thought, "Yeah, that's me," I strongly encourage you to implement the following idea. I know numerous people who have rebuilt bridges by doing it.

an
APPLICATION ▶
to make
Think about the conversations you've killed by making the mistakes described in Chapter 2; then identify one person with whom you'd like to begin again, this time more intelligently. After praying about it, inform that person that you've been reading a book that's caused you to reflect on how you come across in conversations about faith. Ask if he or she would be willing to help you by providing some honest feedback to help you better understand your blind spots in this area.

If you get the green light, ask how it honestly felt to be on the other end of your last spiritual conversation. Listen and take notes, probing to understand what made the person feel this way. When he or she has finished, sincerely apologize for your mistakes. Go the extra mile by asking the person to bring it to your attention immediately if he or she sees you repeat your mistakes.

Of course, what the person does with your attempts to rebuild the bridge is up to him or her. However, when these instructions have been followed in a spirit of humility and sincerity, I have yet to hear of a situation in which God hasn't done some healing in the relationship.

CHAPTER 11

Where the Rubber Meets the Road

Let's do a quick recap before you dive into this chapter. So far we've explored ways to create God Space in our daily interactions with not-yet-Christians—space where God is felt and encountered in tangible ways that address the longings and cries of the heart. We've discussed the importance of balancing listening with wondering—God's teeter-totter—in order to move toward self-discovery and God-discovery. We've learned how to introduce our God stories and God's Word into our conversations in natural ways. We've even explored how to deal with our failures along the way. Now it's time for the rubber to meet the road.

As far as I'm concerned, you've wasted both your time and your money if a book doesn't move you from contemplation to action. It's been said that insight without action is a recipe for despair. We've ended each chapter with practical suggestions on how to move from information to transformation. This entire chapter is devoted to it.

You'll also find answers to some of the most frequently asked questions from fellow Christ-followers who are trying to increase the quality and quantity of their spiritual conversations.

99 WONDERING QUESTIONS

Many times we are never more than a few wondering questions away from a good spiritual conversation. With the right attitude and atmosphere, any of the following 99 questions can be powerful tools. Remember, however, that the best questions always come from the wondering that the Holy Spirit is stirring inside of you as you listen to others. Listening leads to wondering, and wondering provides more opportunities to listen. As you grow in your ability to harmoniously balance God's teeter-totter, spiritual conversations will flow more naturally in your day-to-day life.

Questions About LIFE LESSONS

- I've made it my lifelong goal to learn from others; what's the greatest lesson you feel you've learned so far in your life's journey?
- Tell me about your greatest success and your greatest failure along the way.
- Would you mind sharing with me the greatest piece of wisdom ever passed on to you?

Questions About CAREERS

- What prompted you to pursue your career in _____?
- What do you like most about what you do? least?
- Do you see this as a lifetime career, or a steppingstone to something else?

Questions About TALKING ABOUT GOD

- If someone wanted to talk to you about God, how would you like to be approached?
- Have you ever had anyone approach you and try to talk to you about God?
- What kinds of feelings were you left with after the encounter?

Questions About EVANGELISM

- What images or words come to your mind when you hear the word *evangelism*?
- The word *evangelism* means "to proclaim good news." If that's true, why do you think this word carries so much baggage with it?
- If you were asked to describe the good news that evangelists are supposed to be sharing with people, how would you describe it?

Questions About VOCATIONAL DREAMS

- What is your dream job?
- Are you working toward it already? If not, what is standing in your way?
- What advice would you give to a young person about finding vocational happiness?

Questions About RELIGIOUS EXPERIENCES

- What kind of exposure did you have to religion when you were growing up?
- Why do you think there are so many different religions?
- Do you think it's possible for all religions to be equally right? Why or why not?

Questions About ETERNITY

- What conclusions have you come to concerning life after death?
- Do you think it's possible to be certain about where you'll spend eternity?
- Have you ever explored what the Bible has to say about eternal life?

Questions About A GOOD LIFE

- Have you ever been able to get a handle on what you think your purpose in life is?
- Everyone seems to agree that money by itself can't buy happiness. What, in your opinion, *does* guarantee a happy life?
- In what ways do you feel you're really winning or losing at life?

Questions About BECOMING A CHRISTIAN

- Do you consider yourself to be a Christian?
- Based on your understanding, how does someone become a Christian?
- Have you ever explored what the Bible has to say about how someone becomes a Christian?

Questions About WORLD EVENTS

- How did 9/11 affect your view of God and the world?
- As you've watched or read the news, what conclusions have you drawn about the nature of humanity?
- Do you believe there is a solution to social problems such as rape, murder, famine, war, racism, and divorce?

Questions About GOOD VS. EVIL

- Have you ever had an experience in which you felt the presence of evil?
- Have you ever had an experience in which you felt the presence of God?
- In what ways have you seen good and evil played out in your life?

Questions About BARRIERS TO BELIEF

- What causes you to struggle the most with the idea of God's existence?
- Up to this point in your life's journey, have you met anyone or experienced anything that made the reality of God seem plausible to you?
- To what do you attribute your disbelief in God?

Questions About RELATIVE TRUTH

- It sounds as if you value open-mindedness. Do you ever find yourself closing your mind to certain things, ideas, or people?
- What criteria do you use to determine whether something is true?
- Does your worldview allow for any absolutes?

Questions About MARRIAGE

- How did you meet your husband/wife?
- What have you learned about yourself through marriage?
- What do you enjoy most about marriage? least?

Questions About LOVE

- Has your understanding of the word *love* changed over the years?
- Why do you think so many couples end up falling out of love?
- If you could pass along one word of advice about how to keep a relationship going and growing, what would it be?

Questions About FINDING GOD

- Why do you think so many people prefer to live as if God does not exist?
- What would you want God to do to validate his existence and bring you to belief?
- It's been said that many people never find God for the same reason a robber can't find the policeman standing on the corner; what does this saying mean to you?

Questions About RIGHT AND WRONG

- Some people believe that we are the product of a random evolutionary process. Do you think discussions about right and wrong have a place in that kind of worldview?
- How do/will you teach your kids right from wrong?
- What authority do you appeal to?

Questions About DREAMS

- Did you have any dreams or set any life goals when you were younger?
- What dreams have you let go of?
- What dreams are you still hanging on to?

Questions About THE FUTURE

- Are you optimistic or pessimistic about the future of our world?
- Do you think it's easier or harder to raise kids in today's world than it was when you were growing up?
- What concerns you most when you think about your future?

Questions About MAJOR INFLUENCES

- What experiences have shaped your worldview the most?
- Has there been one book or movie that's left its mark on you in a significant way? How so?
- Besides your parents, is there any one person who stands out as having had a major role in shaping your life? Tell me about him or her.

Questions About GOD'S POWER TO CHANGE US

- God has changed my life; have you ever considered letting him change yours?
- If God had his way with you, what do you think he would change first?
- What scares you the most about letting God change your life?

Questions About TAKING STOCK

- What three principles of life have benefited you the most so far in your life's journey?
- What, if anything, causes you to be hopeful about your future?
- If you had only six months to live, what would be on your list of things to do before you died? Why?

Questions About GETTING TO KNOW YOU

- As people get to know you, what about you do they enjoy most?
- As people get to know you, what about you do they enjoy least?
- As people get to know you, in what area do you feel most misunderstood?

Questions About LEADERSHIP

- How would you describe your leadership style?
- What leadership style do you respond best to?
- Jesus was described as a servant leader. When have you, if ever, experienced that kind of leadership?

Questions About DIRECTION

- Why do you do what you do?
- What life experiences have molded you and motivated you to pursue the path you've chosen for life?
- If you were to choose your path over again, would you choose the same one? Why or why not?

Questions FOR GOD

- If you could ask God three questions, what would you ask?

- If God were to ask this one question, "Are you for me or against me?" what would you say?
- What evidence would you present to defend your response?

Questions About GENDER

- Which gender do you think has the tougher path in life?
- What do you enjoy most about the opposite sex?
- What do you enjoy most about being male/female?

Questions About HATE

- Have you ever hated anyone?
- Has anyone ever hated you?
- Have you ever been able to overcome hatred? If so, how did you pull it off?

Questions About DEATH

- If you could choose the manner of your death, how would you like to go?
- How would you like to be remembered at your funeral?
- Does the thought of death scare you?

Questions About CONTROL

- It's been said that life is largely out of our control. If that's true, why do so many people try to control the uncontrollable?
- Do you struggle with trying to control things?
- What kinds of things do you think can be controlled in life?

Questions About HABITS

- What kinds of habits do you struggle with most?
- Do you ever find yourself doing the very things you don't want to do, or not doing the things you really want to do? If so, what do you attribute this to?
- Have you ever found anything to set you free from this cycle?

Questions About CHILDHOOD

- How would you change the way you were raised?
- What things are you doing/going to do to raise your kids differently?
- What values from your childhood do you want to pass on to your kids?

Questions FOR JESUS

- If Jesus were here right now, what would you ask him?
- How do you think he would answer?
- How would you feel if that happened?

WONDERING INTO ANOTHER CULTURE

In many ways it's much easier to wonder into another culture because our sense of wonder is stimulated by the unfamiliar. The following exercise is intended to serve as a resource for those who find themselves doing missions work in another culture.

- Before you arrive in the country, reread Chapter 6, and look through the 99 wondering questions in this chapter. Discuss the big ideas that you find helpful insofar as they relate to your trip.
- Read the list of 20 questions on the next page. Begin a brainstorming session of things you're wondering about the culture you'll be serving in. Ask someone to keep a running list of these questions.
- After tapping into your sense of wonder, review your list of questions and prepare the ones you think most appropriate.
- As soon as you arrive in your new cultural setting, pair up with another Christian and "wonder around," asking the questions you put together.
- Come back together with members of your faith community to share what you learned.
- Take some time to pray and talk through how to live out Colossians 4:5 in your new cultural setting. My other book, *Irresistible Evangelism* (Group Publishing, Inc., 2003), will give you practical ways to pull this off.

20 QUESTIONS TO STIR YOUR WONDER IN ANOTHER CULTURE

Thanks to Judy Kirkpatrick, the International Internship Coordinator for Athletes in Action, for her contribution to this section.

1. What kind of government does this country have?
2. Who are this country's national heroes and heroines?
3. What languages are spoken here?
4. What is the predominant religion? Are people in this country tolerant of other religions? What is the history of Christianity in this country?
5. What are the most important religious observances and ceremonies?
6. How are animals treated? Do people in this country have household pets?
7. What are the most common forms of marriage ceremonies and celebrations?
8. Do women work outside the home?
9. Is the price of merchandise fixed, or are customers expected to haggle?
10. How do people organize their daily activities—mealtimes, bedtimes, workdays, and so on?
11. What foods are most popular, and how are they prepared?
12. What kind of clothing do most women wear? most men?
13. If you're invited to dinner, should you arrive early, on time, or late?
14. How do people greet one another? How do they take leave of one another?
15. What are the favorite leisure and recreational activities for adults? children? teenagers?
16. What kinds of television programs are shown? What social purposes do they serve?
17. How are children disciplined at home? at school?
18. Are the largest newspapers generally friendly in their attitude toward your home country?
19. What is the history of this country's relationship with your home country?
20. How is evangelization/proselytizing perceived in this culture?

FREQUENTLY ASKED QUESTIONS

As I travel around the world to help God's people live outwardly focused lives in an inwardly focused world, Christ-followers often ask me the following questions concerning spiritual conversations.

"Do you have a surefire transitional question that always works to turn the conversation toward spiritual matters?"

I'm hoping that the answer to this question is evident by now. When memorized transitions are interjected and people realize you're trying to take the conversation somewhere, you'd better hope they actually want to go there. Otherwise, it may be the last spiritual conversation you'll have with them.

If a silver bullet is what you're after, here it is: *Ask for permission.* You will never go wrong anywhere in the world by asking for permission. Doing so demonstrates the gentleness and respect called for in 1 Peter 3:15.

"I can't think on my feet very well, and I'm certainly not an intellectual. How am I supposed to pull off these kinds of conversations?"

The first step I encourage you to take is to become a connoisseur of good questions. Remember: Great questions spark great thoughts and stimulate great conversations. So when you come across a great question, write it down and tuck it away for another day. You'll eventually find yourself interjecting these questions into your conversations at the appropriate times.

Still, you may not always have a ready response. When someone shares a belief that leaves you scratching your head for a response, maybe you could reply this way: "That's an interesting belief. I'm wondering how you came to that conclusion?" Really good questions lead to self-discovery and many times prompt the other person to articulate belief systems they become uncomfortable with even as they're expressing them.

Remember: Great questions spark great thoughts and stimulate great conversations.

Gary Poole's book *The Complete Book of Questions* (Zondervan, 2003) gives you 1,001 questions to prime your mental pump.

Just keep this big idea in mind: The best questions flow from an authentic dialogue and demonstrate that you've been listening. You'll know you're on the right track when you hear comments such as "Wow! That's a great question; I've never thought about that before."

a
SCRIPTURE
to ponder
Second, Proverbs 17:28 says, "Even a fool is thought wise if he keeps silent, and discerning if he holds his tongue." When you're struggling for words, this passage suggests it's best to remain silent. You might say something like "I need to mull that one over. May I get back to you?" Or if you know the question is way over your head, acknowledge that fact. You might ask the person you're talking to if you could invite one of your more "cerebrally gifted" friends to join you sometime in the near future. This will help take the pressure off you and provide the space you need to re-engage in the conversation at your own comfort level.

Finally, I've found it helpful to remind myself that God loves me for who I am and what I bring to a conversation today. He also loves me too much to leave me the way I am. So he puts me into conversations that stretch and prepare me for the future. If you're faithful with the little you think you have to offer in conversation *today*, I think you'll find yourself growing more and more confident and competent to handle more difficult conversations in the future. God promises us in the parable of the talents that we'll be given more when we're faithful with what we have (Matthew 25:14-30).

"I'm afraid they'll ask me questions I won't be able to answer. How should I respond?"

This is actually a great situation to be in because most people are suspicious of people who think they have all the answers. With humility, affirm the person for asking such a great question. Then thank him or her for giving you an opportunity to grow.

If a silver bullet is what you're after, here it is:

Ask for permission.

Sometimes we won't have an answer simply because we don't know enough about the question at hand. If this is the case, ask if the person would be willing to get back together again in a week. This will give you

a chance to do your homework. If you're looking for resources, check out AllAboutGod.com. You might also want to seek out a full-time Christian ministry worker to help you through tough questions.

Other times, we won't have an answer because there isn't one. If someone asks me why God did not thwart the plans of the terrorists on 9/11, I could go into a lengthy discourse on God's sovereignty and man's free will, but at some point the words will begin to sound hollow. If you and I could easily explain questions like this with our finite minds, God would not be God. When you authentically validate your own struggles with the mysteries of life, you build bridges of credibility. Sometimes "I don't know" is not a cop-out; it's a humble acknowledgment that God doesn't come to you for advice.

"What do I do when the person I'm talking to is so resistant/hurt/turned off that nothing I say seems to make a difference?"

I don't know many people who hear truth very clearly when they perceive that the source of their pain stems from God and/or his people. Even if the frustration or anger you encounter started long before you met the person, your attempts at spiritual conversation trigger all those emotions from the past. If the person is extremely resistant, more words just cause more irritation and probably won't make a positive difference. Your only recourse at this point may very well be to pray and serve your way into the person's heart through acts of kindness.

On the other hand, it's possible that if you patiently and sensitively probe to discover the source of pain and frustration, and respond with empathy, a conversation may become viable. For instance, a question like this might get the conversation going: "It seems as if our conversations become very awkward when spiritual matters are discussed. I've been wondering if you've had some negative encounters with God and his people."

If I sense that I may be the source of the resistance, but I'm not sure, I might say something like this: "I sense that I might have said something in our last conversation that caused you to close down. If so, could you help me understand what I said or how I came across? I value our friendship and enjoy our conversations, so if I've offended you, I'd like to make things right."

"None of my not-yet-Christian friends seem to be open to these kinds of conversations. Does that mean I should just leave it alone?"

It's hard to say, because there could be a variety of reasons for this. Start by examining your own heart; maybe you aren't safe enough for such matters to be discussed. If your friends feel they're going to get a moral lecture, they might not want to go there. I think we have to realize that not-yet-Christians can be just as intimidated by us as we are by them.

Once you've done the inner work, though, "leaving it alone" is not an option we should settle for, unless we've been told that spiritual conversation is off-limits. If a "spiritual stop sign" has not been posted, we can respectfully "stir the waters," making it easier for conversation to flow out of the happenings of everyday life. The world around us gives us many natural opportunities to do just that. For example, several years ago the following question would certainly have been relevant: "What do you think about the Christians who are declaring that God allowed the floods to wipe out moral decadence in New Orleans?"

After stirring the waters, I watch and listen carefully for the responses that I get. Engaging in a spiritual conversation without listening is like driving a car blindfolded. Body language and tone of voice many times clue us in on whether to keep going, slow down, or just plain stop. Many times we miss the hints others are giving us because our focus is more on what we're saying than on how they're responding to what we're saying. As we learn to listen, we will wisely begin to start where others *are*—not where we'd like them to be—in our conversations.

"Frankly, the stuff people say about my faith gets me pretty worked up. When I get in that mode, I want to win. How can I learn to back off?"

What do you really get with a win? Even if you are feeling pretty good, you leave the other person feeling like a loser. So you need to remind yourself that winning in a conversation may lead to losing opportunities for future interaction with that person.

I think it's helpful to assess the trigger points that put you in this kind of competitive mode. When you better understand why you get so worked up, you have a better chance of avoiding this kind of an outcome. I encourage you to review your past conversations and look for patterns, topics, or hot buttons

that tend to fire you up. When you identify them, go before the Lord in prayer and ask him to help you sort out what's going on inside you.

This process is essential if you're to live out the truth of 2 Timothy 2:23-25: "Don't have anything to do with foolish and stupid arguments, because you know they produce quarrels. And the Lord's servant must not quarrel; instead, he must be kind to everyone, able to teach, not resentful. Those who oppose him he must gently instruct, in the hope that God will grant them repentance leading them to a knowledge of the truth."

a SCRIPTURE ◄ to ponder

"I listen to my not-yet-Christian friend's objection to Christianity and think, 'He's making a really good point; I've never considered that.' Not only can I not give him an answer, I start to doubt my own faith."

I think we can acknowledge that someone has made a good point without feeling like we've denied Christ. Truth is supposed to surface under scrutiny. It's OK to acknowledge to yourself and to your friend that there are questions about your faith that you've never considered—and to thank him or her for challenging you to dig deeper.

After all, if Thomas had his doubts after being in Christ's presence for three years, it seems more than reasonable that you and I might have a few doubts along the way as well. Many times God uses our doubts as a catalyst for seeking him. As we receive more insight, our capacity to go further and deeper into conversation expands.

"Is it ever OK to say, 'I'm not the right person to talk to you about this,' or 'Having this conversation again is pointless; let's just drop it'?"

This is always an option and a very honest one at that. Conversations move toward being pointless when they end up in an "I'm right; you're wrong" standoff. If you find yourself at this point, it's probably time to change the subject.

Sometimes, however, I want to duck out of conversations due to my lack of patience with the person's seeming inability to grasp the obvious. Rather than "losing my life to find it" by hanging in there during a tough conversation, I find it easier to opt for comfort rather than the cross. I've learned that if the other person is willing, Christ is able to give us what we lack (patience, in my example) to engage in conversation for his sake, not ours.

I'm advocating an honest assessment of what's really driving us to the point of ending a conversation. Even when we come to this conclusion for good reasons, we can still be helpful in other ways. Maybe you know someone who might be better equipped to pick up the conversation and run with it. Just because you drop the conversation doesn't mean you have to drop meeting the needs of your friend. Another possibility is to find a book on the topic of your conversation and use it as the fuel to keep the conversation going.

"Eventually, doesn't it all come down to the fact that you just have to believe?"

Yes, at some point in the process of coming to God, a person does have to cross over from unbelief to belief, but that doesn't mean we should encourage blind leaps into the dark. Josh McDowell used to say, "The heart cannot embrace what the mind rejects as false."

If there is a cerebral impasse that makes the 18-inch journey from the head to the heart difficult, we must respectfully and sensitively come alongside someone with the apologetic that is needed to make belief more plausible.

For many, the missing ingredient at this point is a loving, Spirit-filled Christian community. This will help them to feel the truth, which makes the 18-inch journey a whole lot easier. God often uses our built-in need to belong to make the journey toward believing more tangible.

Having said all that, John 1:12-13 reminds us that true children of God are born from above and not by human decision alone. At some point, our conversations need to move from the horizontal plane to the vertical, as the Holy Spirit is the source of true conversion.

We need to look for signs of the Spirit's work in our conversations. Remember the following tip-offs that a spiritual birth is coming soon and it's time to take on the role of spiritual midwife:

- When people start initiating spiritual conversations and the frequency and depth of their questions increase, God is at work.
- When people express sorrow, dissatisfaction, or fears about their life direction and begin to read the Bible on their own, God is at work.

Your role as spiritual midwife is to help interpret what God is doing in people and to guide them as they take the next step. Words of testimony, specific Scriptures, and prayer can be used mightily by God during the spiritual birthing process. As you "listen in stereo," with one ear toward heaven and the other on the soon-to-be Christian, you'll find the Holy Spirit fulfilling his role as helper quite nicely.

"I'm an introvert, so the whole thought of having a spiritual conversation is very intimidating to me."

I've yet to meet an introvert who never ate or secured a job, or who failed to finish school due to an introverted nature. We all have a built-in drive to accomplish the things we feel are necessary. So I encourage you to take your cue from Moses. When he played the "I'm not very good at speaking" card, God told him to stop focusing on what he could not do himself, and to start focusing on what God *can* do (Exodus 4:10-12). In fact, I've found that introverts have the potential to be the best spiritual conversationalists simply because they are usually better listeners and tend not to dominate conversations.

"Is it wrong to have an evangelical agenda in my conversations?"

As I mentioned earlier, spiritual conversations should be our ultimate motive, not our ulterior motive. When your evangelical agenda begins to drive or dominate the conversation, however, you're taking a big risk. If the person you are conversing with is ready for that agenda, you'll be warmly embraced. If not, there is a good possibility that this will be the last spiritual conversation the two of you will have.

Again, effective evangelism starts where people *are* in relationship to God, not where you would *like* them to be. This will require you to exercise patience and self-control as you journey with them to the cross, one conversation at a time. Your agenda might not reflect God's agenda, so you would be wise to hold on to it loosely.

The key here is to keep in step with the Spirit. "Since we are living by the Spirit, let us follow the Spirit's leading in every part of our lives" (Galatians 5:25, NLT). If there is one thing I've heard not-yet-Christians say again and again, it's that they don't like pushy Christians who are always trying to convert them. If we aren't careful, our evangelical agenda can become more about us than about them. This tends to push people away rather than attract them. Nobody enjoys feeling like a target or someone else's spiritual project.

a
SCRIPTURE
to ponder

"I don't know what to say in most situations, so what am I supposed to do?"

Jesus gave his disciples this principle in Matthew 10:19-20 when he said, "Do not worry about what to say or how to say it. At that time you will be given what to say, for it will not be you speaking, but the Spirit of your Father speaking through you."

It's the "withness" of God that makes spiritual conversations so exciting, if not intoxicating. When we talk to God about people, before we talk to people about God, we can be faith-confident that God will manifest himself in our conversations and make his appeal through us (see 2 Corinthians 5:20). We all must come to a place where we must step outside our circle of confidence and jump into the conversations going on around us with a belief in God's promises.

WHERE THE RUBBER HIT *MY* ROAD

This book might very well have never been written if a young man named Ed hadn't lived out some of these principles in front of me. During my college days, Ed and I had numerous spiritual conversations where he introduced the Bible in very relevant ways. Over a period of several months, God's Word, combined with Ed's conversations, moved me toward God, one conversation at a time. I eventually wrote my story down so I would never forget how powerful spiritual conversations can be. As you read on, imagine someone *you* know who may be just a few spiritual conversations away from having a similar experience through your influence.

MY STORY

Sleeping in on Sunday morning was not an option at my house. I couldn't understand why my parents thought religion was so important. Going to a building with stained-glass windows and singing songs to someone I couldn't see wasn't my idea of a good time. Furthermore, the pastor preached boring messages from a book written thousands of years ago, and we were actually expected to pay for this experience when the offering plate was passed.

For the first 20 years of my life, Christianity seemed like a prison, primarily because it caged me in and prohibited me from having any real fun in life. I partially resolved this torture by using the Jekyll-and-Hyde routine.

Around my parents, I did my best to be the fine young Christian son they wanted me to be, but when I stepped out with my friends, I transformed into the kind of guy no mother could trust her daughter with. On the weekends, I always attempted to be the wildest guy at the parties; likewise, my dating life reflected the typical locker-room attitude of getting as much as possible while giving as little as possible.

I attended a branch campus of Kent State University, where I lettered in basketball and tennis. With only 1,200 students on campus, my popularity, as well as my ego, grew with my success in athletics. I perceived myself as having it all together.

It was time for my bubble to burst, and the girl I had been dating for two and a half years was the pin. After finding out that I had been dating other women, she had the audacity to tell me she wanted to go out with other guys. I snapped! In a fit of rage, bitterness, and jealousy one night, I picked her up and threw her across the room like a rag doll. I stormed out of her house and drove away with a flood of emotions gripping my soul.

For several weeks, I contemplated my existence. For the first time, I realized that my life was a lot like a hot-air balloon—colorful on the outside, but empty on the inside.

When I returned to Kent State for the second semester of my junior year, a Christian group on campus was sponsoring a talk on guy/girl relationships. I figured the least I could do was to check it out. That night I heard things that made sense to me for the first time. I began to realize that my sole source of happiness came from external things, such as sports, girlfriends, and material possessions. Internally speaking, these things brought momentary satisfaction, but no true, lasting fulfillment. I had built my life around things that could be easily taken away. The philosopher Blaise Pascal summed it up best: "There is a God shaped vacuum in the heart of every man which cannot be filled by any created thing, but only by God, the Creator, made known through Jesus."

I began to seek God intensely by reading Christian books, studying the Bible, praying, and asking committed Christians questions about their faith. During the next couple of months, most of my intellectual conflicts with Christianity were dealt with. Now it was time for a heart transplant!

In the quietness of my room one night in 1979, I invited the living Christ to forgive me for my sins and to make me the kind of man he wanted me to be. From that day on, I have seen a progressive transformation of my life

from the inside out. Christ gave my life new direction and purpose. I could now enjoy life without altering my state of consciousness. By God's strength I was able to turn from my pattern of sexual conquest, and remain sexually pure until marriage. My relationship with my parents steadily grew more intimate as I no longer had to hide my lifestyle from them. God gave me a new motivation to go to school and apply the mind he had given me.

Looking back now, I realize that I did not give my life to God that night—I had received a whole *new* life from him. It took me 20 years to realize that Christianity isn't a religion or a bunch of rituals and traditions—it's a personal relationship between God and me through Jesus Christ. May you, too, realize that truth more deeply, and may God use you to bring others to that realization.

FINAL THOUGHTS

Congratulations, fellow sojourner, you've made it to the end. Now that you stand atop the "spiritual conversation mountain," enjoy the panoramic view in front of you.

God Space begins in us when the natural (the flesh) gives way to the supernatural (the Spirit), producing a desire to please our Lord by naturally making the most of our conversations. The Holy Spirit then empowers us to create God Space in our relational encounters by taking the initiative to notice, serve, listen, wonder, and—with permission—share our God stories and bring the Bible into our conversations as the Spirit leads. The results are up to God.

If you are regularly engaging in this process, you'll see an increase in the quantity and quality of your spiritual conversations. You'll also sense God's presence more frequently as you continue to know him and make him known, one spiritual conversation at a time.

So what are you waiting for? The time has come for you to paraglide off this mountaintop with the fresh winds you have acquired. There are some folks back down in the valley who need to experience some God Space, don't you think?

EPILOGUE
The Perfect Fit

Let me share one final story.

In the late '80s, I found myself on a mission trip in Poland, taking one of the most unusual steps of my Christian life. I was 32, and I was "singled out." My grandmother had already moved me off her prayer list and onto her miracle list. In the spirit of James 4:3, I had quit praying selfish prayers and instead had begun to ask God to send my mother a daughter-in-law. But so far nothing had worked.

So I decided to buy a fur coat and ask God to fill it with a woman. Surely such an extravagant gesture would help the Lord see that I was more than ready to meet my mate.

Two years later, I asked Martha Chrouch if she would be willing to change her last name to Pollock. (She really couldn't say no after seeing "the rock" I had purchased to reward her for the right answer!) Before she had much time to think about what she had just done, I asked her to close her eyes and stick out her arms. I pulled out the fur coat, slipped it over each arm, and asked her to open her eyes. It was a perfect fit! I then told her my fur coat faith story. Later that evening, Martha's mom helped me to realize just how faithful God had been. She explained how difficult it is to find clothing for Martha due to her long arms and petite build. This caused us all to rejoice over the "perfect fit"!

Eight months later we walked down the aisle and began our journey into marriage. I was so excited to be married to a godly woman. We pulled out all the marriage books and began to read and study them together. Unfortunately, the more we attempted to make our marriage look like the

ones we read about in the books, the more defeated we felt. We never seemed to get it right; maybe we weren't the perfect fit after all.

After a rough first year of marriage, it finally dawned on us that we were reading books written by people 20 to 30 years into their marriages. It was irrational of us to think that we could attain in one year what had taken them decades to pull off. Can you relate?

As you reach the end of this book, I'm wondering if you might now feel a bit like my wife and I did then, as you compare your spiritual conversations to the ones you've read about. If so, let me remind you that my stories result from 30 years of experience. I've had many failures along the way, despite the perceptions this book may have created to the contrary. In fact, I continue to fall short in the very conversations I'm so passionate about.

But I've learned that it's OK. As I've said before, failure is rarely final or fatal, but simply an opportunity to begin again more intelligently. Embracing failures, or a lack of perceived results, as part of the process will free you up to continue the journey.

God is looking for faithful, available, and teachable people to serve as his "holy matchmakers." He wants to use our conversations to help others meet the eternal lover of their souls. Our role is simply to help others take the next step, one conversation at a time. Whether you have the privilege of introducing them to Christ for the first time, or walking them down the aisle to say "I do" to Jesus, you can't go wrong by being faithful, available, and teachable.

How God uses your conversations is totally up to him. Therefore, success has nothing to do with the results, but everything to do with being faithful, available, and teachable. As apologist Cliff Knechtle puts it, "A person's coming to Christ is like a chain with many links. There is the first link, middle links, and a last link. There are many influences and conversations that precede a person's decision to convert to Christ. I know the joy of being the first link at times, a middle link usually, and occasionally the last link. God has not called me to only be the last link. He has called me to be faithful and to love all people."

So relax, be yourself, and let the Holy Spirit have his way in your relational connections. Resist any notion of turning the pages of this book into a formula. You will serve God best by talking to him about how to apply the

kingdom principles in this book to your day-to-day life. Always leave the results up to him!

How God uses your conversations is totally up to him.

If you're willing to persevere in this holy endeavor, your words and actions will eventually flow out of the changes God has brought about in you. When God sees that you're faithfully creating God Space in your everyday life, he will arrange relational encounters for you because he knows you will direct others toward the Bridegroom. Only when they say "I do" to him will they truly experience the perfect fit!

CONTACT ME

I have committed my life to guiding God's people into living outwardly focused lives in an inwardly focused world. If you have found this book helpful in your journey, and you would like me to come help your faith community discover its own God Space, please don't hesitate to call me at 937-289-4422, or e-mail me at doug.pollock@athletesinaction.org.

Before you do, please visit my website: GodsGPS.com. There you'll find helpful resources as well as information about how to bring me into your faith community to speak or conduct workshops. I would consider it a privilege to serve you in any way I can.

Come and Experience...

GOD|SPACE

at

LIFETREE CAFÉ ℠